NEW HAVEN

John Warner Barber's Eastern View of the Public Square or Green, *in New Haven, Conn., published in 1840, shows the wooden fence that was replaced by the current fence of iron and stone in 1846. Courtesy, New Haven Colony Historical Society.*

NEW HAVEN
An Illustrated History

Edited by Floyd Shumway and Richard Hegel
Pictorial research by Lucinda V. Burkepile

Sponsored by the New Haven Colony Historical Society
Windsor Publications, Inc., Woodland Hills, California

Library of Congress Cataloging in Publication Data

New Haven: An Illustrated History

    Bibliography
    Includes index.
    1. New Haven (Conn.)—History. 2. New Haven (Conn.)—
Description. I. Hegel, Richard. II. Shumway, Floyd. III. New Haven
Colony Historical Society.
F104.N65N48   974.6′8   81-65217
ISBN 0-89781-033-3   AACR2

Printed in the United States of America

Editors: Lissa Sanders, Phyllis Rifkin
Picture Editor: Teri Davis Greenberg

CONTENTS

INTRODUCTION

The publication of *New Haven: An Illustrated History* represents the culmination of more than a decade of planning. The necessity for a scholarly and profusely illustrated history has long been recognized. The enthusiastic reception in 1976 of the New Haven Colony Historical Society's excellent but smaller and limited in scope *Graphic View of New Haven* reinforced the need.

The chapters of this book have been prepared by recognized scholars. They provide a well-researched history of New Haven arranged in both chronological and subject chapters.

The outstanding editorial assistance of Anne Wilde and general planning assistance of Richard Ballard are deeply appreciated. The guidance of the New Haven Colony Historical Society's President, Mrs. Frank Clayton Hepler, has been invaluable, as has been the support and advice of the Society's Publications Committee Chairman, Mr. John O. C. McCrillis. Mrs. Ottilia Koel, the Society's Librarian and Curator of Manuscripts, has been most supportive in all aspects of the research.

And, finally, we wish to pay our respects to the business enterprises and institutions without whose support as "Partners in Progress" this book would have been impossible.

Floyd M. Shumway
Richard Hegel

Chapter I
NEW HAVEN, 1638 TO 1690

by Thomas J. Farnham

It is a long way from the parish of St. Stephen, Coleman Street, London, to New Haven on the shores of Long Island Sound, especially if one were to travel by way of the Netherlands and Massachusetts Bay. Nevertheless, there must be a beginning to any tale; and the story of New Haven begins properly at St. Stephen's.

On October 5, 1624, 74 householders of the parish, one of only three in London that could elect its own clergy, met to choose a vicar: John Davenport. Born in 1597, the fifth son of a respectable but modest family, Davenport attended the Free Grammar School in Coventry and Magdelan Hall, Oxford, although he failed to complete his degree there, "not from any want of time, or of willingness, or of sufficiency (as was well knowne in Oxford), but from want of meanes (my friends being unwilling) to keepe me longer at the University." He then found employment as a private chaplain to a gentry family living in northern England and later as a lecturer at the Church of St. Lawrence, Old Jewry, London. His first real charge came at age 27 when he went to St. Stephen's.[1]

While Davenport was considering his new responsibility, James I ordered the Bishop of London, George Montaigne, to examine accusations that the young clergyman was a Puritan. Convinced that the Church of England was in desperate need of reform, Puritans had once hoped that James might encourage a simpler form of Protestantism; but he had been king only a short time before demonstrating that he had no tolerance for dissent. Davenport denied the charges, vigorously asserted his orthodoxy, and was duly inducted into the vicarship of St. Stephen's.

Doubts continued to circulate about his religious positions, however. His insistence that the clergy be educated brought him into disfavor with the High Church Party then forming around William Laud, who in 1628 succeeded Montaigne as Bishop of London. When Charles I seemed about to appoint Laud Archbishop of Canterbury and to give him full authority to crush dissent within the Church of England, Davenport saw only one course open to him; he would abandon England and seek sanctuary abroad. Laud's appointment came on August 4, 1633; Davenport left London on August 5. There was no need to ponder the matter further.

Eventually making his home in the Netherlands, Davenport read glowing accounts of New England from his friend John Cotton, formerly of Boston, Lincolnshire, now of Boston, Massachusetts Bay. Davenport decided to move again, this time back to England but only to remain there long enough to prepare for his eventual move to the New World. Believing that God was about to punish England for its manifold and persistent wickedness, he

The Reverend John Cotton's descriptions of New England influenced John Davenport's decision to emigrate to the New World. Cotton's biblical code of laws, written for the Massachusetts Bay Colony but never adopted there, became the framework for New Haven's first government. From Ellis, Arthur B., History of the First Church in Boston. *Boston: Hall and Whiting, 1881.*

hoped to organize a saving remnant of that nation's population and to find refuge in New England, where these saints could prepare for Christ's return and the final judgment.

Davenport's scheme was ably abetted by Theophilus Eaton, whose father had earlier baptized Davenport in Coventry and who had once been Davenport's playmate in that textile

community. Since then Eaton had risen to be deputy governor of the Eastland Company, the commercial agent of James I to Denmark, and the agent of Christian IV of Denmark in London. An original patentee of the Massachusetts Bay Company, Eaton was a man of wealth, an able administrator, and a zealous Puritan.

Together Eaton and Davenport organized a company of parishioners from St. Stephen's and families from the counties of Kent and Hertfordshire and prepared for the move to New England. The business agreement that bound these persons together has long since disappeared, so one cannot say if their original intention was to form a plantation of their own or to incorporate with Massachusetts Bay. If Davenport and Eaton had planned to build their new Zion in Massachusetts Bay, they soon changed their minds, for that colony had been the scene of repeated challenges to Puritan orthodoxy, the most important coming from Mistress Anne Hutchinson; the two emigrants had had enough of doctrinal disputes. Also, of particular interest to Eaton, was the lack of commercial opportunity in Massachusetts. Those harbors that might be capable of handling a brisk trade were already in the hands of aspiring merchants. If the new Zion was to have a solid commercial base, then it would have to develop elsewhere.[2]

While they were pondering these difficulties Davenport and Eaton learned of the "rich and goodly meadows of Quinnipiac." Men like Captain Israel Stoughton and Captain John Underhill had happened upon the Quinnipiac River region while pursuing the Pequot Indians, the scourge of the Connecticut River settlements. Their reports of a splendid harbor excited Eaton and Davenport. By the end of August, Eaton and a handful of men had set out from Boston to examine the source of these tempting reports.[3]

What Eaton found delighted him. Not only were the meadows of Quinnipiac "rich and goodly" and the harbor magnificent, but the hinterland appeared also to be a likely source of beaver pelts and other furs, which could add an important economic dimension to the colony. The location of Quinnipiac was ideal for taking advantage of the market the Dutch in New Amsterdam provided. Eaton may well have spent the winter on the Quinnipiac. Clearly a few men—tradition sets the number at seven—remained from September until April, 1637–1638, on Long Island Sound. If Eaton was not present, Joshua Atwater was probably left in charge.

Seven months to the day after Eaton and the advance party left Boston, Davenport and about 500 followers set sail for Long Island Sound. They arrived at the site of the party's camp on April 24, 1638. They hoped to create a Christian utopia on the banks of the Quinnipiac; Christian in the sense that the church would provide the force to hold the community together and utopian in the sense that the community was to live in perfect unity, perfect peace, and perfect order. Only a few would be selected to join the new Zion, and from these select few would be demanded complete loyalty.

But if the founders of New Haven dreamed of a Christian utopia, they also envisioned a commercial empire that would certainly control all of the Long Island Sound and possibly the coastline as far south as Delaware Bay. To New Haven came the wealthiest group of merchants to come to any New England settlement before 1660; they hardly intended to spend their lives raising Indian corn and peas. These men came to make the most of Quinnipiac's spacious harbor and favorable location.

The Quinnipiac settlers had no authority to settle on the lands that they had chosen, but because the area fell within the grant made by Robert Rich, Earl of Warwick, to certain friends of Davenport and Eaton, the two men believed their position could be made secure. To compensate for their lack of title, they negotiated with local Indians a series of treaties, each of which the Englishmen obtained for "twelve coats of English trucking cloath, twelve alcumy spoons, twelve hatchetts, twelve hoes, two dozen of knives" as well as promises of protection. These treaties, dated November and December 1638 and May 1645, ceded the Indians' rights to what is now New Haven, East Haven, Branford, North Branford, North Haven, Wallingford, Cheshire, and parts of Orange, Woodbridge, Bethany, Prospect, and Meriden.[4]

The Quiripi dialect of the Quinnipiac Indians was studied and transcribed by the Reverend Abraham Pierson of Branford. His catechism, written in both Quiripi and English, is thought to be the first work of an author from the Connecticut colonies printed in this country. Courtesy, New York Public Library.

Even before these agreements had been made, the settlers began to prepare their new home. What the advance party had accomplished is unknown, but it is hardly likely that it remained idle during its seven months in the wilderness. But as much as it might have completed, there was seemingly endless work to be done. The settlers had to clear land, build homes, establish fences, plant gardens, construct roads and bridges, and, first of all, lay out a town.

The identity of the man who designed the town that would one day be called New Haven is a mystery, but it might have been Lion Gardiner, a friend of Davenport; the similarities between his plan for Saybrook and the design of New Haven are striking. Gardiner was an acknowledged military engineer, town planner, and architect. Or possibly the planner was Robert Seeley, who had been acquainted with Davenport and Eaton since the days of St. Stephen's. He had the technical qualifications as well as sufficient status within the company of settlers to be considered for the task. More than a decade later, in 1651, Eaton called upon him to help with the "settling and moulding of the Towne" which New Haveners planned to build on the banks of the Delaware River. Elizabeth Brown, in a forthcoming article in the New Haven Colony Historical Society *Journal*, argues convincingly that John Brockett, who is frequently designated as the man who laid out the town, probably had little if anything to do with the scheme.[5]

The designer, whoever he might have been, organized the town around 11 squares, nine of these divided from a half-mile square rectangle; and two, called suburbs, which extended from the rectangle to the waterfront. At the center of the nine squares was the marketplace. Nothing was especially original about the town's plan. Similar arrangements already existed in old England, in Cambridge in the Bay Colony, and in several towns of the Connecticut River Colony.

Within these 11 squares were the homelots of those settlers, called proprietors, who had originally invested in the association. The extent of their lots depended upon their wealth and family size. Householders, the settlers who had no financial stake in the venture, received small lots outside the 11 squares. Thirty-two families belonged to this category. The homelots eventually contained the family homes as well as necessary outbuildings. Here also would be found gardens, poultry yards, and even livestock, for two years would pass before the town parceled out substantial tracts of farm acreage.

The earliest dwellings were at best crude. Michael Wigglesworth, who came to Quinnipiac when he was about seven, later described these quarters: "Winter approaching we dwelt on a cellar partly underground covered with the earth the first winter. But I remember that one great rain brake in upon us and drencht me so in my bed being asleep that I fell sick upon it; but the Lord in mercy spar'd my life and restored my health."[6]

These rude quarters quickly gave way to the type of homes the settlers had known in England, houses of heavy timber construction, in some cases the spaces between the timbers being filled with wattled twigs and clay. But the seasonal range of temperatures was twice as great in New Haven as in England, and the consequent expansion and contraction caused the clay to crumble and fall out. The answer to this problem was handsawn clapboards which soon became the common sheathing material.

New Haven settlers built homes on a scale appropriate to their status. Some were opulent, "great estates" according to Cotton Mather. Others were humble. Theophilus Eaton lived, as one historian has stated, "in baronial splendor in the largest of all houses in New Haven." Davenport also lived grandly having in his home "many apartments and thirteen fireplaces," according to Ezra Stiles. Both these households were maintained by black slaves. These grand houses were possible because the wealthy Quinnipiac settlers brought large amounts of cash with them. Probably Quinnipiac had more ready money at its inception than any other New England town. For the same reason, no starving time haunted the settlement; cash meant adequate provisions.[7]

Thus far the Quinnipiac planters lacked a carefully defined political agreement. Certainly they had drafted some form of business contract before they invested the £36,000 that the venture required. A plantation covenant also had been drafted in Massachusetts to provide additional political organization. Nevertheless, until a government was created, Davenport and Eaton ruled in large measure by dint of their own prestige. Such an arrangement was hardly sufficient for these Puritans who dreamed of creating the perfect society.

At the center of their community would be the church. Because they believed in original sin and in predestination, they anticipated that few persons would ever find salvation. Only the elect then should be church members, but the common good demanded, they argued, that all should live a Christian life; laxity would violate God's law and could lead to destruction, as Sodom had been destroyed. Thus the community charged each Puritan with watching not only his own behavior but that of his neighbors as well. The church was then both the nurturer of individual faith and a means of social control. The church was the cement of society; and in Quinnipiac, which represented New England Puritanism at its most fastidious, the state existed to enforce Puritan conformity and morality.

So the first step in organizing the community was to establish a church. This process began on June 4, 1639, at Robert Newman's barn where the 70 proprietors met and agreed that only church members should be allowed to vote or hold office. This decision was a victory for Davenport, who believed

in the separation of church and state but feared political control by wealthy but godless laymen, over the Reverend Samuel Eaton, who argued for a broader franchise. Then the proprietors selected 12 (later reduced to 11) men who were to choose seven of their own number to create a church. These Seven Pillars, as they were designated, included both Eaton and Davenport, the latter also being selected pastor, a position he would hold until 1668. On August 22, 1639, the church began to function, the first services being held outdoors or in Newman's barn. By 1640 a 50-foot-square meetinghouse complete with tower and turret stood on the marketplace. The town had provided £500 for its construction.

The congregation granted church membership carefully. It was available only to those whose claim to conversion was convincing, and only the children of such persons were entitled to baptism. But everyone was expected to

The first meetinghouse on the Green was completed within two years of the colony's founding. Poorly designed and constructed, the walls soon began to buckle under the weight of the roof. From Lambert, Edward, History of the Colony of New Haven. New Haven: Hitchcock and Stafford, 1838.

attend church and to support it financially.

On October 25, 1639, the Seven Pillars assembled once again. They formed themselves into a General Court, a legislative and judicial assembly, added nine other persons to their number, and then chose from among themselves a magistrate and four deputies, each to serve for one year. Eaton, not surprisingly, became magistrate, a position he would hold until his death in 1658.

The government these men would lead was based largely on biblical law; but it was biblical law as seen through the eyes of the Reverend John Cotton of Boston. He had specifically modified the laws of Moses for use in the Bay Colony. Named by Governor John Winthrop "Moses his Judicialls," the Cotton plan never achieved adoption in Massachusetts but became, as far as it was applicable, the framework for the new Quinnipiac government. The criminal sections of the Cotton code related closely to scripture, the civil sections, to existing practice in both England and Massachusetts.

In November the deputies ordered the creation of a trained band of soldiers. Military training was necessary not only to cope with possible threats from nearby Dutch and Indian enemies but also to provide a diversion that was as unrelated as possible to the temptations of the flesh. Davenport urged his followers to "abandon your carding, dicing, chambering, wantoness, dalliance, scurrilous discoursing, and vain spinning out of time" and to attend to military drills. As dangerous as the Dutch might be to the infant plantation, the devil within was, in Davenport's eyes, always the greatest danger.[8]

Until this point called Quinnipiac, the settlement became New Haven (actually Newhaven) on September 1, 1640. The General Court apparently selected the name both to honor the English town in Sussex—although none of the settlers appeared to have come from that town—and to describe the new harbor which was now their home.

To prepare future generations for service to both God and the commonwealth, New Haveners were quick to establish schools. When in 1642 the proprietors established a free school (free in the sense that it was open to all who could pay tuition), Ezekiel Cheever, one of four men in the settlement who had attended either Oxford or Cambridge, agreed to serve as its first master. In 1656 New Haven required all parents and masters to provide schooling for children and apprentices to allow an understanding of the Scriptures; and in 1668, thanks to the bequest of Edward Hopkins—a wealthy merchant in the original Davenport-Eaton party that came to Boston—The Hopkins Grammar School received its first students in the school-house on the marketplace, by then called the Green.

From the first, the founders of New Haven believed it essential to create a network of subsidiary towns whose function would be to deliver agricultural and forest products to New Haven for trade with other ports. In 1639 the Reverend Peter Prudden took a band of Hertfordshire settlers down the coast to establish Milford. The same year the Reverend Henry Whitfield founded Guilford, and two years later the Reverend Richard Denton brought a group of dissatisfied Wethersfield persons to Stamford; 1641 also witnessed the establishment of Southold on the eastern end of Long Island. The Reverend Abraham Pierson settled Branford in 1644.

In addition to the communities which sprouted around Long Island Sound, the Delaware Company—organized by George Lamberton, Robert Newman, Nathaniel Turner, Eaton, and Davenport—in 1640 bought land on Delaware Bay from the Indians and sent about 50 families to the area to exploit the fur trade of the region. On October 31, 1641, New Haven extended its control over the region.

To cope with its expanded territories, the town of New Haven on Oc-

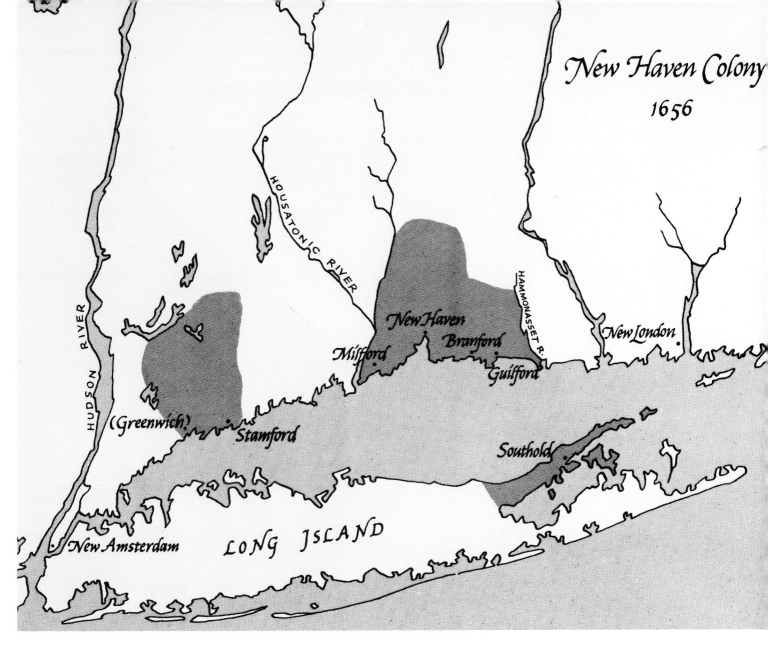

HUDSON RIVER

HOUSATONIC RIVER

New Haven
Branford
Milford
Guilford
HAMMONASSET R.
New London

(Greenwich)
Stamford
Southold

New Amsterdam LONG ISLAND

tober 27, 1643, formed the New Haven Jurisdiction, sometimes called the New Haven Colony. Composed of six towns—New Haven, Branford, Milford, Guilford, Stamford, and Southold—the new jurisdiction was an expanded version of the town government, even to the point of allowing only church members to vote or hold office. The New Haven Jurisdiction, along with Massachusetts Bay, Connecticut, and Plymouth, sent delegates to the recently formed New England Confederation, although it would be an exaggeration to suggest that New Haven carried the weight in that body that the great Bay Colony or even Connecticut did. As the distinguished scholar Rollin Osterweis has pointed

out, "the town preceded the colony, dominated the colony, and survived the colony."[9]

By 1641, New Haven possessed a population of about 350 adult householders, 250 children, and 200 servants, a 60 percent increase over the number that had arrived only two years before. Most of these persons came from eastern England—London, Hertford, Kent, Essex, and Suffolk, in particular— and the Midlands, especially Buckingham. The population was a young one, probably half the adult residents being no more than 30 years of age. Yet almost all the adults were part of a family group, no bachelor class existing.

Not only was the population nu-

The New Haven Colony, outlined on this map by John O. C. McCrillis, included three separate geographic areas. Stamford and Southold merged with the Connecticut Colony and New Haven was forced to follow suit in 1665. (NHCHS)

merous; it was also talented. Eight or nine men were men of great wealth, and the community contained a disproportionately large group of international merchants. The concentration of merchants was to be expected in a community that anticipated becoming a thriving commercial center.

During its first years, New Haven's trading patterns were simple. New arrivals brought with them plenty of cash which they used to purchase seed corn, livestock, and essential provisions; the established residents used the cash to purchase manufactured goods from England. Prosperity lasted as long as the steady flow of immigrants continued to arrive.

But eventually the supply of newcomers began to decline, and dreams of a commercial empire began to fade. The Quinnipiac hinterland proved to be barren of fur-bearing animals. Thus the outpost on the Delaware became even more important. But at this point the Dutch joined forces with their neighbors in New Sweden to drive the New Haveners back to Quinnipiac. The Delaware fur trade was to belong to the Dutch until the Duke of York seized New Amsterdam in 1664.

More and more New Haven watched its trade with the outside world move through Boston. In a valiant attempt to open direct trade with England, New Haven, cut off on the south and west by the Dutch who were not especially eager to trade with their neighbors up the Sound, assembled enough local produce to fill one large vessel. Possibly built in New Haven, this "Great Shippe," carrying local provisions and also the colony's hopes for a commercial base, set sail in January 1646. The ship was never heard from again. Along with the vessel, a cargo

valued at £5000, two of the magistrates—Thomas Gregson and Nathaniel Turner—George Lamberton, the wife of Stephen Goodyear, and the ship's crew also disappeared. The disaster was both personal and economic.

The loss of the ship, combined with the failure of the Delaware Company, was the death blow to hopes of making New Haven important commercially. Direct trade with England remained only a fantasy; and instead of becoming the center of a network of supplier towns, New Haven itself became a satellite town for New Amsterdam and Boston. New Haveners had to survive on agriculture in an area particularly ill-suited for farming. By 1680 the town's home fleet consisted of merely five vessels, only one of which was capable of anything more than the coastwise trade. As Samuel Maverick explained, "the merchants either dead or come away, the rest gone to their Farmes, The Towne is not so glorious as once it was." Indeed it had become "little else than a colony of discouraged farmers."[10]

In the late 1650s New Haven seemed to find a solution to its economic problems. The younger John Winthrop discovered iron ore in the bogs between New Haven and Branford. New Haven merchants saw the discovery as an answer to their prayers and, with the assistance of grants from both the town and the Jurisdiction, established a furnace in the eastern part of town. They even managed to persuade Winthrop to move to New Haven and to supervise the operation. But before the project was really off the ground, Winthrop abandoned New Haven to become governor of the Connecticut River Colony. Unexpected costs began to appear, and although the industry continued to drag on until the early

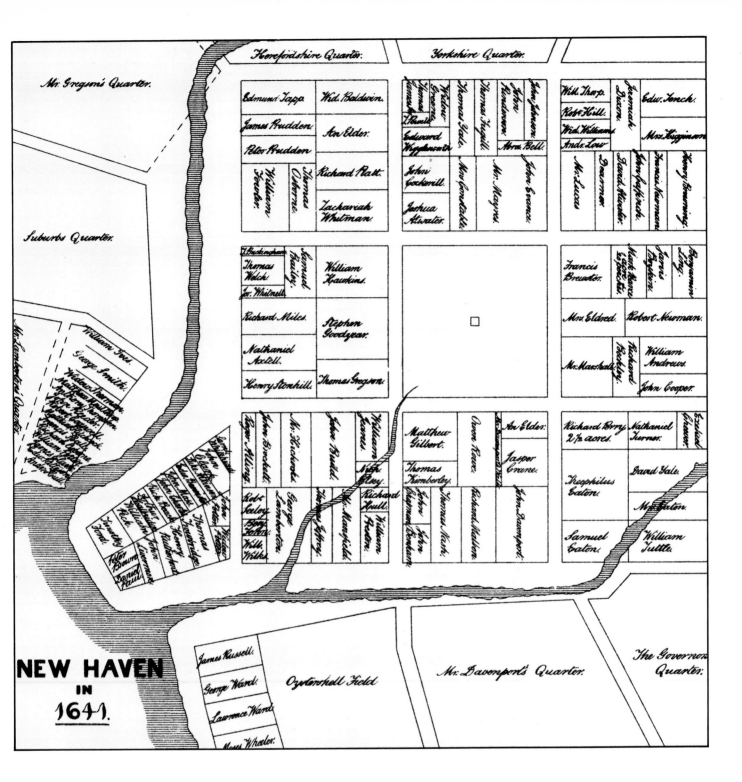

NEW HAVEN IN 1641.

Mr. Gregson's Quarter.

Herefordshire Quarter.

Yorkshire Quarter.

Suburbs Quarter.

Edmund Tapp. / Wid. Baldwin. / James Prudden / An Elder. / Peter Prudden / William Fowler / Thomas Osborne. / Richard Platt. / Zachariah Whitman.

T. Buckingham / Samuel Bailey / Thomas Welch / Jos. Whitnell / William Hawkins. / Richard Miles. / Stephen Goodyear. / Nathaniel Axtell. / Henry Stonhill. / Thomas Gregson.

John Johnson / Edward Wigglesworth / John Cockerill. / Joshua Atwater. / Thomas Yale / Mr. Constable. / An Elder / John Evance. / John Brockett / Mr. Richbirck / John Budd / William Ives / Nich. Elsey. / Richard Hull / Matthew Gilbert. / Thomas Kimberley / Robt. Seeley / George Lamberton / Richard Osborne / William Manfield / Owen Rowe / Richard Malbon / Peter John / Richard Beckam / Jasper Crane. / John Davenport.

Will. Thorp. / Robt. Hill. / Wid. Williams / Andr. Low / Mr. Lucas / Mrs. Higginson / Pearman. / Josiah Diron. / Edw. Tench. / Mrs. Higginson / Henry Browning. / Francis Newman. / David Atwater. / John Gibberd. / Francis Brewster. / Mrs. Eldred. / Robert Newman. / Mr. Marshall / Richard Beckley / William Andrews. / John Cooper. / Richard Berry 2½ acres. / Nathaniel Turner. / Theophilus Eaton. / David Yale. / Mr. Eaton. / Samuel Eaton. / William Tuttle. / Ezekiel Rowe.

James Russell. / George Ward. / Lawrence Ward. / Moses Wheeler.

Oystershell Field

Mr. Davenport's Quarter.

The Governors Quarter.

1660s, the ironworks proved to be more a liability than an asset.

Thus agriculture remained the way of life in New Haven, but the settlers were not, for the most part, experienced farmers. They also mismanaged their livestock. New Haven cattle were smaller and inferior to New Amsterdam cattle, although Dutch traders acknowledged that they did "fat and tallow well." Hogs were more likely to thrive on New Haven's sparse pastures than cattle. But they were a nuisance. Town law required that they be kept at least five miles from the marketplace during the growing season (many fields were two miles from the town's center). The swine refused to cooperate, and the already inadequate crops suffered further from the creatures' nocturnal excursions.

The crafts fared almost as badly in

The "Brockett" map of 1641 is primarily useful for its delineation of New Haven's colonial plan of nine squares and two "suburbs." This copy of the map was made in 1880; the original vanished shortly thereafter. (NHCHS)

early New Haven as did agriculture. Workmanship was frequently shoddy. The first meetinghouse, for example, was so poorly designed that its walls could not support the weight of its roofs. The walls bulged badly. Repeated attempts to shore up the building were finally abandoned in 1668, and the town built a new structure. The town accused tanners of spoiling hides "for want of skill or experience in the tan of this country" and found it almost impossible to locate an honest and efficient miller.

While Puritan New Haven was failing to become the utopia its founders had envisioned, Puritanism in England was thriving, and by 1649 Oliver Cromwell's Puritan followers were in control of England's government. In fact by 1647 the great Puritan migration to New England had reversed itself, and some of New Haven's most talented residents returned to the mother country. William Hooke, Davenport's assistant at the church and later Lord Protector Oliver Cromwell's household minister, noted that goods were in short supply at the time of his departure from Quinnipiac and stated that "we and our posterity, now almost prepared to swarm forth, are confined and straited, the sea lying before us and a rocky rude desert, unfit for culture and destitute of commodity behind our backs."[11]

The departure of many neighbors, the repeated economic setbacks, and the realization that utopia was not to be—at least not on the banks of the Quinnipiac—created tensions in New Haven that made the town less appealing than during the early years of exuberance. These tensions were aggravated by the fact that only those who could describe a convincing account of salvation could become church members. All others were denied not only communion and the right to have their children baptized but also participation in the political life of New Haven.

People began to speak out against New Haven's leadership. In 1645 George Ward questioned some of Davenport's financial interests. Luke Atkinson brought up the same embarrassing question in 1647. By the late 1640s, such individual protests had coalesced into political opposition to the clumsy leadership of Davenport, Eaton, and other aristocratic officials. The exclusiveness of their control might have been tolerated had their leadership been more effective, but New Haven had faltered under these men, and henceforth the so-called Younger Party would be a factor to be considered. The conservatives reacted to these challenges by demanding even more conformity. In 1656 the colony adopted Governor Eaton's revision of the old "Moses his Judicialls." The revised version was even more uncompromising than the original. Jury trial continued to be unknown. On the Sabbath, labor and travel were taboo, but so also were cooking, bedmaking, shaving, and kissing one's own children. The code prohibited at all times card playing; the celebration of Christmas and saint's days; dancing; the playing of any musical instruments except the drum, trumpet, and jew's harp; and mince pies. To question the colony's ideology was punishable by death.[12]

An unhealthy concern over sexual matters, especially the lapses of others, developed in New Haven. In 1666 New Haveners conducted a lengthy discussion of sins possibly committed by young persons among the Indian corn at harvest time. In the end the town decided to prohibit unmarried persons from wandering about in the cornfields after 9:00 p.m. unless accompanied by a parent, master, or some authorized person.

After 15 years in office, the arrogant but devoted Eaton died in 1658, and in 1660 New Haven learned that the English Puritan cause had collapsed and the Stuart monarchy was again in power. Davenport initially denied the reports, but eventually he had to acknowledge the accession of Charles II. The Restoration reminded New Haveners that they had no legal basis for either the town or the New Haven Jurisdiction. But even in the face of this crisis, New Haven failed to respond with a single voice. Davenport and his conservative followers were ready to fight to maintain New Haven's independence. The Younger Party, on the other hand, urged union with Connecticut which offered a more liberal franchise and a more relaxed religious atmosphere. William Leete, now governor of the New Haven Jurisdiction, was the leader of the Younger Party and an advocate of union.

Davenport and his fellow conservatives resisted the idea of proclaiming allegiance to the new king so long that when the proclamation finally did come, in August 1661, its effect was merely to remind Charles of New Haven's tardiness. At the same time, New Haven welcomed Edward Whalley and William Goffe, two of the men who had signed the death warrant of Charles I in 1649. The two resided in Davenport's home during March 1661. Even had the old minister's behavior been more diplomatic, New Haven's fate was probably sealed. When the younger John Winthrop, then governor of Connecticut, went to London to seek a charter for his colony, New Haven asked him to obtain a single document establishing the legitimacy of both the Connecticut Colony and the New Haven Jurisdiction. Winthrop managed in May 1661 to secure a single document but one that defined New Haven as part of Connecticut.[13]

In October 1662 Davenport ha-

Here Lieth   The Body
of the Honorable
WILLIAM LEETE
Governour of the
Colony of New Haven
and after the union,
of Connecticut.
He died April 16
1683.
Aged 72 years.

rangued a New Haven General Court into refusing Connecticut's "evil" demand for unity. A year later Davenport was even more unbending, because by that time Connecticut had accepted the Half-Way Covenant which allowed both partial church membership to any baptized adult who led a decent life and baptism for the children of such persons. Davenport denounced this as the work of the devil. He persuaded the General Court to appropriate £300 to secure a separate charter from the crown. The appropriation was too late. Southold had already seceded from New Haven and joined Connecticut. Stamford followed suit, and several persons from Guilford "tended themselves, their persons and estates" to Connecticut. Some Milford residents also began to question the narrow orthodoxy of New Haven. Only New Haven under Davenport and Branford under Pierson held firm.

In 1664 Charles granted to his brother James, Duke of York, all lands

PURSUING THE REGICIDES

The pursuers of Goffe and Whalley, the Judges of Charles I. passed over a bridge near NewHaven, Con. while the Judges were concealed underneath

A 19th-century engraving by John Warner Barber depicts the agents of Charles I pursuing Whalley and Goffe. New Haven's citizens helped them to escape. From the Barber Collection, NHCHS.

between the Delaware and Connecticut rivers; and in August of that year, the Duke's forces captured New Amsterdam. The possibility of independence for New Haven disappeared. Now its choice was rule by the Catholic duke or union with Connecticut. On January 7, 1665, New Haven ungraciously surrendered "as from a necessity brought upon us."

The act of union was more than Davenport could bear. His life's work, he lamented, had been lost. He vowed to leave New Haven and in 1667 accepted the invitation of Boston's First Church to become its minister. From that bastion he hoped to lead a Puritan counterrevolution. But in Boston his life was surrounded by strife and controversy, 17 ministers of the Bay Colony finally condemning Davenport for deceptions he had perpetrated on the First Church. On March 15, 1670, he left "a troublesome unthanckfull evill world."[14]

With the departure of Davenport, the New Haven church nearly collapsed. The congregation neglected to find a replacement for its first minister, and apathy flourished. When New Haven finally mustered enough energy in 1684 to invite James Pierpont to become its minister, he agreed to accept the charge only if the church adopted the Half-Way Covenant. One would think that this change in doctrine would have been welcomed in New Haven. Church membership had fallen off drastically since early days. Even among those who were the leading citizens in town in 1665, only half were church members; obviously church membership was no longer a prerequisite for leadership in New Haven. But if after 1665 fewer men belonged to the church, certainly more could vote. Connecticut did not limit the franchise, as had the old New Haven Jurisdiction, to church members. Instead those persons who owned real estate of a value of £20, were at least 21 years old, were willing to swear the Freeman's Oath, and were known to be persons of peaceable behavior and civil conversation were eligible.

All these changes came too rapidly for some New Haveners. A short time after New Haven's incorporation into Connecticut, William James, Robert Treat, and others began negotiations with Philip Carteret, Lord Proprietor of New Jersey, for a site on which to settle, and by 1673 some 85 families removed to Newark to preserve the old ways of Puritanism.

New Haveners also moved north, to Wallingford, established in 1670, and Derby, founded five years later. The men who led the push to the north were different from those who had originally established Quinnipiac or its satellite towns. By the late 1660s, the founders had been discredited and had disappeared as a class. The rank and file were also different. The population was now more provincial, not as well educated, less cultivated, coarser, poorer, less adventuresome, and less devout than the founders; and they were more committed to their own selfish interests. For example, when in 1675 New Haven faced the threat of King Philip's uprising, the town's people responded not by building fortifications but by haggling among themselves over who should do what and who should pay for what.

The utopia that Davenport and Eaton had envisioned years before in London had failed to materialize. To a large degree, Eaton and Davenport and the other leaders of early New Haven were themselves responsible. Men of talent, but also convinced of their own righteousness, they sought what was clearly beyond their reach. Their judgments were frequently faulty. Eventually their leadership was repudiated, and their faltering experiment, now merely a poor and sleepy farming community with a tiny fleet of "five small ships," sought a new identity within Connecticut. But as any Puritan would admit, the impulse toward human perfection was bound to fail. So with early New Haven.

The Reverend James Pierpont's 29 years of ministering to New Haven's spiritual needs were highlighted by his participation in the rules for church discipline which became known as the Saybrook Platform. In 1698 he married Mary Hooker, who was born in Farmington, Connecticut, in 1673. She was his third and last wife, outliving him by 26 years. (NHCHS)

Guilford's Henry Whitfield returned to England in 1650. His massive stone house, built in 1639, is now a museum administered by the State of Connecticut. (NHCHS)

Chapter II

FROM PURITAN VILLAGE TO YANKEE CITY, 1690 TO 1860

by Dorothy Ann Lipson

The United Church on the Green was photographed about 1910 by Myron W. Filley. The Whitehaven Church, formed as a result of the Great Awakening, was divided in 1769 when a group of its members seceded to form the Fairhaven Church. In 1796 the two congregations reunited and in 1884 the Third Congregational Church was absorbed. The United Church on the Green resulted from the consolidation of these congregations. (NHCHS)

To read the *Town Records* for the first century considered in this chapter, it would seem that New Haveners were largely concerned with electing such officers as fence-viewers, leather-sealers, and haywards; dividing up the town lands and deciding where the roads should go; regulating the meanderings of stubbornly presumptuous cattle, swine, and geese; and waging a long and deadly battle against barberry bushes.[1] In fact, as part of the British empire and, later, of the new American nation, New Haven's economic, social, and political concerns were always framed by larger, distant events and the processes of modernization that characterized Western societies.

New Haven's history from 1690 to 1860 seems to roughly divide into three periods. First, from the 1690s through the first half of the 18th century, New Haven was a colonial village, moving beyond the spoiled dream of a Puritan commercial polity to become a relatively self-contained agricultural community. Then, from about 1750 through the Revolutionary period and until the century's end, the history of New Haven is that of a growing town, a story of economic and political reorganization. Finally, from about 1800 until the eve of the Civil War in 1860, rapid growth, increasing heterogeneity, and industrialization marked the modernizing city.[2]

Puritan Village: 1690-1750. At the end of the 17th century New Haven was the village center of a predominantly agricultural township, even if its spacious central market, the Green, might remind the inhabitants of an earlier, grander vision. It was the county seat and, after 1701, the co-capital (with Hartford) of the colony. In a population of about 1,500, only some 150 were freemen, qualified to vote and hold office. About 150 clapboard houses, some of them painted blue and most of the rest left to weather, ringed the Green. Near the center of the Green stood the town's single church, presided over by its hard-working and scholarly minister, the Reverend James Pierpont. There was fishing and oystering at the harbor, and a few small vessels for coastal trading. Farming stretched inland from the harbor, toward borders as yet not fully explored.[3] It was a relatively static community.

On May 3, 1689, news of England's Glorious Revolution reached New Haven from Massachusetts, to which Connecticut had recently and unwillingly been bound in the Dominion of New England. A "Declaration of the Gentlemen, Merchants and Inhabitants of Boston and the Country Adjacent" informed New Haveners of the accession of William and Mary and warned that King William's War (1689-1697) with France had already involved

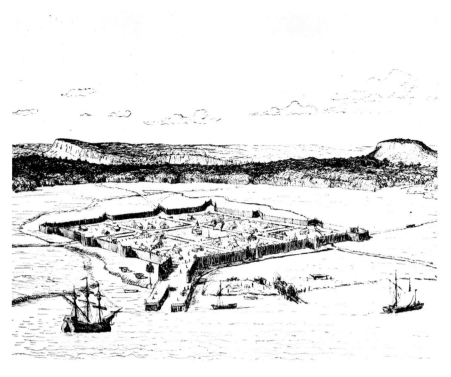

MAJ. GEN. DAVID WOOSTER.

Dav. Wooster~

the colonies in "the Perplexities of another Indian War" on the Canadian border. Pending directions from England, Massachusetts had imprisoned the Royal Governor of the Dominion, Sir Edmond Andros, and reorganized according to her pre-Dominion government. The New Haven Town Meeting immediately followed suit.

New Haveners were prayerfully conscious that they were at a "Daungerous Juncture" in imperial affairs, but they were also determined to prevent "Anarky and Confusion" in the face of the French threat. Town watches were set up under military control, the town garrisoned and fortified, a "flying Army" outfitted, and contingency plans made for a "Dragoone Company" to be ready "in Case of any Inroad or assult." From time to time throughout the next few years New Haven men marched off to take part in the frontier raids and sorties as the Connecticut militia fought beside the English army.

New Haven's immediate and independent response to the threat of war in 1689 set the pattern of her participation in the Anglo-French wars of empire that lasted until 1763, when France lost her North American colonies. During Queen Anne's War (1701-1713), 350 New Haveners marched

with the English army in the Connecticut levy to help defend the northwestern frontiers or seize Nova Scotia. During King George's War (1739-1748) young David Wooster was among the New Haven militia in the colonial force that captured Louisburg in 1745. When Louisburg was exchanged for Madras, India, in the peace negotiations, New Haveners had an immediate experience of the sacrificial role of colonial interests in England's imperial chess game.

Around the middle of the 18th century, heralded by frontier clashes with both the French and Indians, war resumed as the Seven Years' War (1756-1763). Although all efforts to achieve concerted action among the colonies had been unsuccessful, the colonial militia had acquired considerable experience and authority. Nathan Whiting and David Wooster marched over familiar terrain at the head of experienced contingents of New Haveners in the British attack on Crown Point. The long years of French and Indian warfare also helped to train up a new kind of colonial leadership: well traveled on the colonial frontiers, tested in war, and smarting at their subservience to the regular English army and to English imperial priorities.

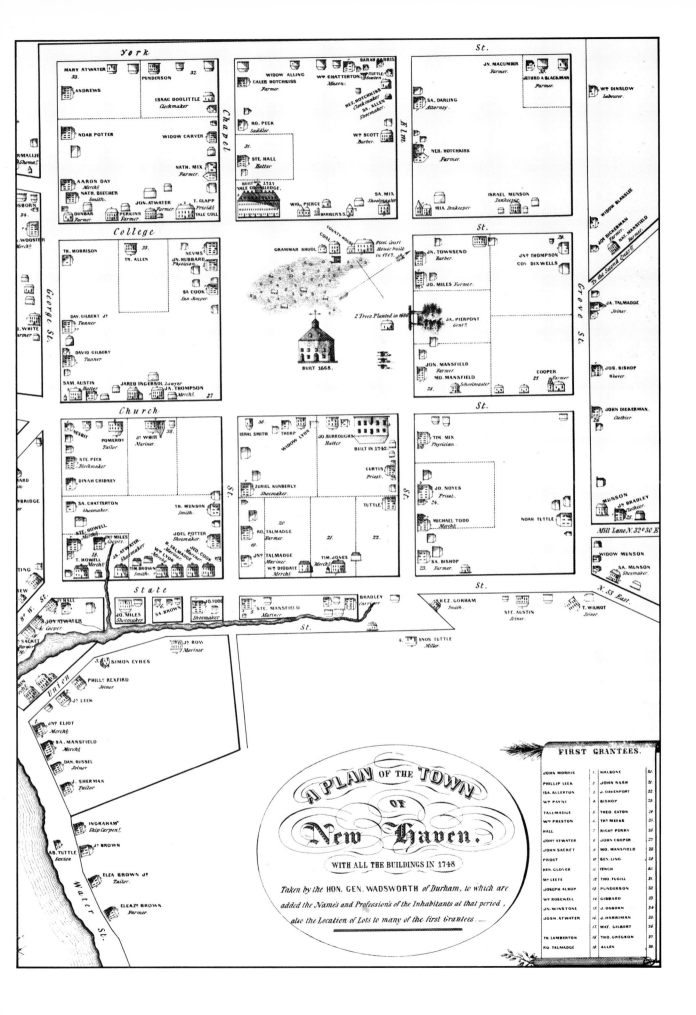

A PLAN OF THE TOWN OF New Haven.

WITH ALL THE BUILDINGS IN 1748

Taken by the HON. GEN. WADSWORTH of Durham, to which are added the Names and Professions of the Inhabitants at that period, also the Location of Lots to many of the first Grantees.

FIRST GRANTEES.

JOHN MORRIS	1.	MALBONE	20.
PHILLIP LEEK	2	JOHN NASH	21
ISA. ALLERTON	3	J. DAVENPORT	22
Wᵐ PAYNE	4	BISHOP	23
TALLMADGE	5	THEO. EATON	24
Wᵐ PRESTON	6	THᵒ MEEKS	25
HALL	7	RICHᵈ PERRY	26
JOHᵗ ATWATER	8	JOHN COOPER	27
JOHN SACKET	9	MO. MANSFIELD	28
PROUT	10	BEN. LING	29
HEN. GLOVER	11	TENCH	30
Mʳ LEETE	12	THO. FUGILL	31
JOSEPH ALSOP	13	PUNDERSON	32
Wᵐ ROSEWELL	14	GIBBARD	33
JNᵒ WINSTONE	15	J. OSBORN	34
JOSH. ATWATER	16	J. HARRIMAN	35
	17	MAT. GILBERT	36
THᵒ LAMBERTON	18	THO. GREGSON	37
RO. TALMADGE	19	ALLEN	38

31

The changing role of the colonies in the first half of the 18th century and the constant anxiety of frontier warfare may have contributed to a period of intense religious revival in the 1730s and 1740s, known as the Great Awakening. This movement was a product of the Puritan belief that a specific, describable experience of divine grace was necessary for conversion and for church membership. Many of the churches in New England, like the one in New Haven, had originally been such gathered communities of "visible saints" who could testify to such experiences. By the end of the 17th century, however, the churches of New England believed that they were experiencing a serious decline of religion. In 1708, delegates from the churches in Connecticut and trustees of the newly organized Collegiate School (Yale), James Pierpont prominent among them, tried to reverse this decline. They formulated the Saybrook Platform, to regulate the church through periodic regional meetings of ministers and lay leaders. These councils decided all questions of religious orthodoxy, buttressed by the legal authority of the General Assembly which conferred on local communities the right to tax the inhabitants for the support of their ministers. In addition, the steady spread of the Half-Way Covenant, designed to enlarge church membership by allowing infant baptism and offering nominal membership to everyone of good character, also undermined the local authority of the saints. The Great Awakening was, in part, a reaction to the regulation and formalization of religion through the Saybrook Platform and the Half-Way Covenant.[4]

The Great Awakening in New Haven was unexpectedly tumultuous. When the Reverend Joseph Noyes was ordained in 1716, New Haven's only church seemed stable and harmonious. Noyes, the son-in-law of Pierpont, was an early graduate of the Collegiate School. He had been instrumental in bringing the college, renamed Yale, to New Haven, a source of local pride and prestige. By the late 1730s, however, groups of church members calling themselves "New Lights" began actively to oppose the Half-Way Covenant and the Saybrook Platform, which "Old Lights" like Pierpont and Noyes had accepted. They demanded churches composed of saints, and "converted" ministers who could evoke religious experiences similar to their own in their congregations. In New Haven, as elsewhere, the confrontation of the Old and New Lights soon split the church congregation and changed the religious map of the community.[5]

In the 1740s a famous English revivalist, George Whitfield, toured New England. Others followed, who attacked the Half-Way Covenant and the unregenerate or "lifeless" ministry in churches governed by the Saybrook Platform. In New Haven the Reverend James Davenport, great-grandson of John Davenport, "speaking with his heart on fire," came to confront the quiet conservatism of Noyes's ministry. The church soon divided between New Lights and Old Lights. Whitehaven Church was formed and by 1759 had sufficient membership to legally warrant the division of the First Church's property. Jonathan Edwards the Younger was ordained there, but he too presided over further doctrinal splintering. Meanwhile, enough New Haveners had returned to the Church of England to require a minister of their own. By the middle of the century the homogeneity of religious life in New Haven had been significantly eroded.

Throughout the wars and religious upheavals of the first half of the 18th century, New Haveners continuously and methodically divided their land, creating pressure of a new kind. The founding English merchants had bought 13 square miles around a beautiful harbor in exchange for some yard goods and assorted cutlery, because they were interested in trade. But New Haven had developed into an agricultural rather than a commercial town. As historian Rollin Osterweis succinctly put it, "An inadequate labor supply and an absence of good markets dampened the ardor of commercially minded citizens and a currency lacking elasticity and uniformity discouraged them." Then too, as families multiplied, a demand to explore, divide, and settle the common lands grew. Seven divisions of the land before the middle of the 18th century occupied a great deal of time and thoughtful energy. However, with her lands distributed and divided

the English armies in the hinterland. In 1755 James Parker began to publish commercial news in Connecticut's first newspaper, *The Connecticut Gazette*. New public buildings, like the enlarged brick Statehouse, grew up around the Green. Most important of all, a group of "new men" with commercial ambitions came to New Haven and quickly shared authority in town affairs with the long-settled landed elite.

into new towns, New Haven seemed effectively blocked from further expansion, both by England's mercantile regulations and by imperial frontier land policies. The bonds of empire had begun to chafe.

Revolutionary Town: 1750-1800. From 1756 to 1763 New Haven had participated importantly in the far-flung theaters of the Seven Years' War. Her men marched overland to Lake George and Canada, and her ships and sailors went to the Caribbean. Roger Sherman, a merchant newly come to new Haven, served as Commissary for the colony's forces, and New Haven's harbor came to new life as a transportation center. The village took on the look of a commercial town. The wharves were enlarged and lengthened to take care of increasing traffic. A post office was established in 1754 to handle the mail of

After the French and Indian wars, when England tried to recoup some of the costs through the Stamp Act, New Haven became one of the centers of colonial opposition. Jared Ingersoll, a prominent lawyer and town leader, became the Stamp Act Collector for the colony. Ingersoll had been in London, acting as Connecticut's agent, when the Stamp Act was passed. Although he had opposed its passage, he accepted the appointment as Collector "to be of service" at a difficult time. Returning to New Haven in May of 1765, Ingersoll was dismayed to find how high feelings ran. Crowds paraded the streets, gathered in front of his house, and burned his effigy. Just before the semiannual meeting of the General Assembly, the Freeman's meeting voted unanimously to ask their representatives to "use their ut-

The earliest surviving view of the city is this 1786 woodcut that served as the masthead for the New Haven Chronicle, *published by Daniel Bowen. (NHCHS)*

Republican President Thomas Jefferson invoked a storm of controversy when he appointed Samuel Bishop to replace Federalist Elizur Goodrich as collector of the Port of New Haven. Bishop, an eloquent opponent of the Stamp Act during the Revolutionary War, and his wife, Mehitabel Bassett, sat for these portraits by Reuben Moulthrop circa 1800. (NHCHS)

most Endeavors" toward repeal.

The General Assembly was not so unanimous in its opposition to the Stamp Act as New Haven had been, but the vote to send delegates from Connecticut to a Stamp Act Congress did carry. By the next session of the legislature the political Old Lights, who tended to be more patient with constituted authority, were supplanted by the political New Lights, who were less inclined to accommodation. The political Old and New Lights shared many philosophical attitudes. For example, they were both opposed to the exercise of arbitrary power by the British, even while they both were afraid of the popular disorders that might be unleashed by defying legitimate au-

thority. The important difference between them, according to historian Richard Bushman, *From Puritan to Yankee, Character and the Social Order* (p. 265), was that the New Lights came from that Puritan tradition which "had always held that governmental power was limited and that God sanctioned resistance when liberty was usurped." New Light convictions about individual freedom had their base in religious attitudes that were politicized in Connecticut by the Stamp Act crisis.

In New Haven many of the new men, like David Wooster, Roger Sherman, Benedict Arnold, James Hillhouse, and Samuel Bishop, were New Lights in politics as well as religion. During this period they moved into the

lead in New Haven politics. When all business ground to a halt with the boycott of articles or procedures requiring stamps, they were instrumental in getting the town to vote to continue business as usual—without stamps. As Samuel Bishop formulated it for the *Town Record*, "The Stamp Act is unconstitutional and therefore not binding on the Conscience." The town was justified in ignoring the demands of empire. "We have already bravely gone too far to retreat: If we remain firmly united . . . if we are fit for anything but the Chains of Slavery, if we have the Spirit of a Free People, the most threatening Danger cannot shake us." Such rhetoric was revolutionary.

The Stamp Act was repealed in February 1766, announced by triumphant church bells, but the British government immediately began a new and comprehensive program of American taxation. Boston took the lead in resisting British economic regulation by adopting a self-denying policy for importations. The New Haven town meetings in 1769 followed their lead by finding that "it is expedient for the Town to take all prudent and legal Measures to encourage the Produce and Manufactures of this Colony, and to lessen the Use of Superfluities, and more especially . . . articles imported from abroad." New Haven, along with other colonies, had declared economic war. Military operations were not far behind.

Right
*Roger Sherman's contribution to
the Constitutional Convention in
Philadelphia was known as the
"Connecticut Compromise." His
plan called for two Federal legislative bodies. Representation in
the lower house would be based
on population, but each state
would have equal representation
in the upper house. We know
these bodies today as the House
of Representatives and the Senate
of the United States. From the
Mitchell Collection, NHCHS.*

Facing page
Top
*Black Rock Fort, erected during
the Revolutionary War, was later
renamed in honor of martyr Na-
than Hale. The foreground of
J. W. Barber's 1836 view shows
Fort Hale's battery in ruins.
From the Barber Collection,
NHCHS.*

Bottom left
*Benedict Arnold, one of the most
active of New Haven's West Indies merchants, employed his
maritime skills against the British on Lake Champlain and then,
after changing sides, against his
former countrymen in Connecticut. From the Dana Collection,
NHCHS.*

Bottom right
*Not all New Haveners were in
favor of the Federal Constitution
which Roger Sherman had helped
to draft. Attorney Abraham
Bishop, shown here in a portrait
by Reuben Moulthrop, vigorously opposed its adoption.
(NHCHS)*

In 1774 the Boston Tea Party aroused the colonies to concerted action. Roger Sherman, representing his fellow townsmen as well as the colony of Connecticut, was sent to the first Continental Congress in Philadelphia. There he signed the Articles of Association— the first of four agreements that documented the history of the American Revolution. (In later years he was to sign the Declaration of Independence, the Articles of Confederation, and the Constitution, lending a New Haven presence to the whole national epic.) But he was back in New Haven, and on April 21, 1775, when the alarm of the Battle of Lexington reached the town, New Haven mobilized at once. For example, the arrogant, impetuous young merchant, Benedict Arnold, insisted on marching north the next day at the head of about 50 members of New Haven's Second Company of

Footguards. Within a year Arnold was planning to lead an American expedition against Quebec, and during the war he became a hero at the Battle of Saratoga. Then in 1780, with his attempted betrayal of West Point, he became the arch-villain of the Revolution. When Arnold marched off to Lexington, however, most of his fellow townsmen cheered him on. The town formed two new companies of militia, fortified the harbor with breastworks and a battery at Black Rock, and placed a warning beacon at the harbor. By November of 1775 New Haven had essentially declared for revolution by voting in Town Meeting that anybody who felt bound to support the laws of England or could not take up arms against the King, should be requested to leave town "peaceably." By July 4, 1776, 13 colonies in North America were similarly committed.

MAJ. GEN. BENEDICT ARNOLD.

Right
The house and outbuildings belonging to the farm of Amos Morris were burned by invading British troops in 1779. Legend has it that Amos and his large family were reduced to living in a chicken coop capriciously spared from the flames. Morris rebuilt his home, but his fortune had been dealt a blow from which it never recovered. (NHCHS)

Three eventful years after the Declaration of Independence, the beacon lights at New Haven Harbor and the guns at Black Rock warned that the English were about to invade. Most families gathered up their valuables and retreated to the hills and woods. The militia mobilized hastily and tried to harry the pincer movement that landed overwhelming English forces in West Haven and New Haven. William and Thomas Chandler, Tory sons of Joshua Chandler, a prominent lawyer, guided the invaders to the center of town. According to a contemporary account, "The town being now in full possession of the enemy, it was . . . delivered up, except in a few instances of protection, to promiscuous plun-

der." The English soldiers found the stores of West Indian rum, while the officers and "loyal gentlemen" of the town banqueted at the Chandler house on one end of the Green. The next morning the British forces left, prudently accompanied by those who had identified themselves as Tories before or during the raid, and went on to harry the coast at Danbury and Norwalk. In their wake, New Haven mourned its dead and captured, rebuilt its wharves and houses, and, with a cautious eye to the harbor, carried on for the remaining years of the war.

In 1783, two years after the final battle at Yorktown, but before the peace had been formally signed, New Haven began to reorganize politically

for the dawning national era. A city charter was granted by the General Assembly in 1784. (At about the same time East Haven, North Haven, Hamden, and Woodbridge were incorporated as separate towns, paring down New Haven proper to approximately its present shape.) The new town government consisted of a mayor, four aldermen, and a council of 20, all ultimately responsible to the traditional Town Meeting. A Mayor's Court was empowered to deal with civil cases within the city and a host of new offices were created to better order city life and to regulate commercial transactions.

As part of New Haven's design for economic growth, immigration was encouraged by the town, which had in colonial times carefully guarded its residents and freely "warned out" transients. For example, in 1784 almost immediately after the charter was granted, the city voted to readmit to citizenship "such Tories as are of fair character and will be good and usefull members of Society." At the same time, a distinguished city "Committee of Hospitality" was set up "to assist all such strangers as shall come to the city for the purpose of settlement therein." A decade later the New Haven Chamber of Commerce, one of the first in the country, pioneered in private and civic assistance to commerce and industry, and New Haven stood poised on the threshold of unprecedented urban growth.

Above
In 1776, at the meeting of the first General Assembly of the State of Connecticut, several New Haven men petitioned the legislature to remove two Tory leaders from their town. One of them was Ralph Isaacs, a prosperous merchant who responded by moving to Branford, where he died in 1799. These portraits of Isaacs and his wife Mary Perit were painted in happier days by William Johnston. (NHCHS)

Facing page
Between 1825 and 1828 James Hillhouse superintended the building of the Farmington Canal which provided a waterway from the coast in New Haven to Northampton, Massachusetts. Ironically, the railroad pictured on this broadside of 1845 proved a more reliable means of transport and the canal suspended operations three years later. (NHCHS)

Below
Turnpikes to Litchfield, Derby, Milford, and Hartford connected New Haven to an expanding highway system that stimulated commerce and travel. This tollboard from the Derby Turnpike was retired in 1907 when the road became a public highway. (NHCHS)

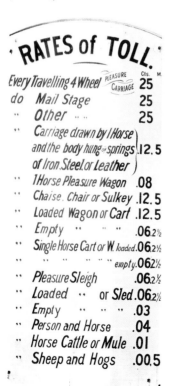

Yankee City: 1800-1860. When James Brewster, a leading New Haven industrialist, reminisced in the middle years of the 19th century about life in New Haven around 1800, the changes in his lifetime had been so rapid that he knew he recalled a completely different era. New Haven in 1800 had contained between four and five thousand souls, including about 115 free blacks and some 85 slaves. There were three churches, two Congregational and one Episcopal, although there were also at least seven Methodist and seven Catholic families, and one each of Baptist, Quaker, Moravian, and a few other denominations. During the War of 1812 this religious profile was made visible in the three new church buildings on the Green, which to this day symbolize traditional New Haven.

Life in New Haven in Brewster's youth had been slow and circumscribed. People walked or rode on horseback or in wagons. There was only one "taxi" in the form of a dilapidated hack, and only two or three families were rich enough to maintain carriages. Fishing boats and coastal and West Indian vessels filled the harbor until the embargo and the War of 1812 deterred all but the most adventurous smugglers. Money was scarce and property and labor were cheap. On Chapel Street, land cost about $35 a front foot. Skilled mechanics might aspire to as much as $6 a week in wages, but laborers received about $3.50. With beef at seven cents a pound and butter at eight cents, good lodging for the single worker, including meals and laundry, could be found for between $2.50 and $5 a week, but very little was left over for other needs. However as Brewster recalled, "There were many enterprising young men at that day just commencing business life," and many of them were destined to become the leaders of an increasingly industrial New Haven.

One of the basic changes that encouraged and accompanied industrialization was known as the transportation revolution, because the modes and

pace of travel were so radically altered in so short a time. During the 17th and 18th centuries New Haven's broad harbor and the rutted post roads along the coast and inland to Hartford were the main routes of commerce. In the early years of the 19th century the uncertain wind power of sails was replaced by steam, and turnpikes spread across the state like lacework.

A revolution in the techniques of production accompanied the transportation revolution. The development of Eli Whitney's "American System" of manufacture is described in another chapter, but its importance to the industrial future of the area—and, indeed, the country—cannot be overstated. During the first half of the 19th century New Haven's skilled craftsmen became industrial mechanics, and the city began to send its small arms, garments, tools, and other products to the markets of the world.[6]

Rapid changes in all aspects of life obviously affected New Haven's ideas and attitudes about the world around them. There were greater differences in wealth and in religious and ethnic allegiance than there had ever been. There were greater social problems and increased anxiety about how to deal with them. Moreover, the new state constitution of 1818 marked the end of the hegemony of the Congregational churches of Connecticut. It is against this background that the Second Great Awakening in Connecticut should be considered.

Although the Second Great Awakening, like the first one, involved periodic revivals and an intensification of individual religious conviction, its lasting legacy was in the growth of an evangelical clergy and laity who tried to stem the tide of religious indifference and control mounting social evils through voluntary associations. As historian Charles R. Keller summarized the movement, "First there were revivals and missionary activities, and then came Bible, tract and educational societies, Sunday schools, attempts at moral reform, and humanitarian endeavors."[7] Through these church efforts, women were organized for the first time in ways which permitted a wider social activism. The work of the Awakening can be seen in organizations like Noah Webster's Society for the Inspection of the Common Schools; the New Haven County Temperance Society, headed by such town leaders as Simeon Baldwin and David Daggett; the General Hospital Society of Connecticut (later Yale-New Haven Hospital); and a myriad of "young men's" and "female" support groups for self-help or do-good. A new demand for civic improvement led to increased fire and police protection, paved and lighted streets, improved civic architecture, and the development of the New Haven gas and water supply by private companies. Most important of all, the evangelical impulse at the beginning of the 19th century helped focus attention on the fundamental social issue of antebellum America: the question of slavery and the future of black Americans.

Slavery had existed in New Haven since the days of Davenport and Eaton, but slave labor had never been an important part of its economy. In the reforming atmosphere of the Revolution, Connecticut had passed a Gradual Emancipation Act, and in 1788 had prohibited slave trade. In 1790 the "Connecticut Society for the Promotion of Freedom and for the Relief of Persons unlawfully holden in Bondage" began to meet annually to hear such abolitionist speakers as the Reverend Jonathan Edwards the Younger, Noah Webster, Theodore Dwight, and Ezra Stiles. The Reverend Leonard Bacon, Charles Ingersoll, Roger S. Sherman, and Simeon Baldwin helped form a local chapter of the American Colonization Society. The African Improvement Society, with racially mixed leadership, organized the United African Congregation and a community school. However, there were few radical abolitionists. Most people seemed indifferent, at best, to the aspirations of the black community which formed the lowest socioeconomic group in the city.

NEW HAVEN AND NORTHAMPTON
DAILY
CANAL BOAT LINE,
AND
STEAMBOAT TO CHEAPSIDE.

The New Haven and Northampton Canal Transportation Line have extended their line of Boats to Cheapside, by adding a Steamboat to run from Northampton. They have also a Steamboat running in connection with the above line from the Basin Wharf in New Haven to New York.

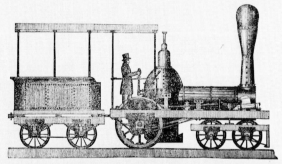

By this arrangement Goods shipped from Albany and Boston by the Western Railroad via Westfield Depot, and from New York and the South via New Haven, will arrive at Cheapside with safety and regularity in the best deck Canal Boats.

The Steamboat Franklin will leave Northampton for Cheapside landing, on **MONDAY, WEDNESDAY,** and **FRIDAY.** Returning, leave Cheapside landing on **TUESDAY, THURSDAY,** and **SATURDAY.** The Steamboat **SALEM** will leave the Basin Wharf in New Haven for New York, every **MONDAY** and **THURSDAY** at 9 o'clock P. M. Returning leave Old Slip, New York, every **TUESDAY** and **FRIDAY,** at 5 o'clock P. M. For freight or passage inquire of *J. & N. BRIGGS,* No. 40 South Street, New York, or of *N. A. BACON,* New Haven, or of the Captain on board.

Freight from Boston and Albany will be delivered daily at the Brick Depot, Westfield, and transhipped without delay in the canal boats for Northampton and Cheapside landing, near Greenfield, and in connection with

BEECHER'S DAILY LINE FROM NEW HAVEN,

In 1831 the Town Meeting voted 700 to 4 against the establishment of a Negro college in New Haven. By the end of that decade, however, the *Amistad* Affair dramatically changed the public attitude.

On September 1, 1839, a United States coastal patrol boat brought into New Haven harbor, as the nearest port with a United States District Court, the Spanish schooner *Amistad*, which the patrol had taken possession of near Montauk Point, Long Island. Imprisoned on the ship were about 50 Mendi warriors, their young and handsome chief, Cinqué, and two Cuban plantation owners. It appeared that the Mendis had been captured in Africa and taken to Cuba by Spanish slave traders. The plantation owners bought them and were transporting them to another port in Cuba when the Mendis mutinied. They captured the vessel, killed the captain and cook and, after the crew had fled, tried to force the owners to sail the *Amistad* back to Africa. Instead, the Cubans had zig-zagged in coastal waters, hoping for just such an opportunity as the appearance of the United States coastal patrol presented.

The Mendis were brought to the County Jail on Church Street, and a steady stream of antislavery leaders visited them. The prisoners' daily exercise period on the Green soon drew curious and admiring crowds from all over the city. The exotic warrior tribesmen, so unlike New Haveners' conception of downtrodden slaves, gave the city an opportunity to envision the African heritage of its own black population and to contrast it with that population's disadvantages. While community understanding of the antislavery impulse grew, the owners, the officers of the American "salvage" ship, and the Spanish government fought over possession of the *Amistad* and its passengers until a Supreme Court decision returned the Mendis to Africa in 1842. By the election of 1860, even though New Haven's town politics had been dominated by local Democratic leadership, there was just enough nationalist and antislavery sentiment to give Lincoln's Republican party a 128-vote majority in the three-way ticket that split 6,154 votes among the Republican and the Northern and Southern Democratic parties.

By the mid-19th century the City of New Haven had assumed a modern shape. Its population had increased eightfold, doubling between 1830 and 1860. It was no longer ethnically and religiously homogeneous because great waves of immigration to America had brought many newcomers to New Haven as Connecticut's chief receiving port. An 1861 map plots nine Congregational, five Episcopal, four Methodist, two Baptist, and two Roman Catholic churches and one Jewish synagogue. Even the appearance of the town had changed. Busy streets and sidewalks intersected a thoroughly tamed and tended Green and radiated toward an increasingly complex and rapidly moving system of transportation.

The whole teeming town had been beautified by the work of James Hillhouse and a pioneer group of urban planners who had, among other things, lined the streets with elm trees. Charles Dickens in his *American Notes* caught the spirit and design of New Haven's arching "natural ornaments"; they seemed, he said, "to bring a kind of compromise between town and country; as if each had met the other halfway, and shaken hands upon it." They helped veil the uglier aspects of industrialization. But the greatest change in New Haven was in the attitudes of its people—in ideas about progress through commercial and industrial innovation and improvement through civic and social action. A famous photograph of Temple Street around 1860 shows a deceptively serene arcade of elms in front of the three churches on the Green. Under these elms New Haven men were about to march off to a Civil War that not only confirmed the nationalist implications of the American Revolution, but also marked "the final surrender of traditional society."[8]

THIS DIPLOMA WAS AWARDED

by the

NEW-HAVEN COUNTY AGRICULTURAL SOCIETY,

Above

The horrors of the slave trade were vividly brought home to New Haven's citizens during the trial of the Amistad captives. The ship, which the Mendi tribesmen had hoped would return them to Africa, is the subject of this anonymous watercolor, painted sometime after 1839. (NHCHS)

Left

Agricultural fairs were held on the Green from 1833 to 1856. The New Haven County Agricultural Society awarded this premium to Mr. William Bradley of Hamden in 1845 for a pair of working oxen. (NHCHS)

Chapter III

THE RISE OF METROPOLITAN NEW HAVEN, 1860 TO 1980

by Ira M. Leonard

Change seems the defining characteristic of 19th- and early 20th-century New Haven. A secondary trading community during the colonial era, New Haven's economy was also shaped by—and its physical landscape dotted with—dozens of small craft and tool shops. These local manufacturing and processing industries had developed as adjuncts of the seaport trade and commerce. New Haven's decisive shift from a mercantile and manufacturing economy to an industrial one, however, dates from the 1830s. By 1850 the Wooster Square section of New Haven was the manufacturing center of the town. The shift in economy was reflected in a shift of local life away from the waterfront and harbor to the New Haven Green, the city's historical center, which by the 1840s had become the business and government center.

Expanding economic opportunity during the 1830s, 1840s, and 1850s attracted a diversity of people to the city, among whom were New England farm boys and girls, Europeans of Irish and German descent, who entered the United States through New York or Boston, and native-born Afro-Americans. New Haven's population jumped from 10,678 in 1830 to 40,000 between 1850 and 1860. The newcomers' labor constructed the transportation-communication links, factories, and shops, and without it the Elm City's economy

would not have developed so quickly or been so productive. Most of the newcomers were unskilled or semiskilled laborers for whom the promise of upward mobility went unfulfilled for many years, but opportunity seemed unlimited for those few individuals with entrepreneurial experience, occupational skills, capital to invest, and drive; they were able to start their own businesses, shops, or stores.

Population growth generated economic opportunity and also social problems and tensions within the city. By 1860 New Haven's 40,000 people were crowded into 4,500 smallish dwelling places, and for the first time the city experienced congested living conditions. The low wages paid to the laborers who worked within New Haven tended to magnify difficulties. Girls and women who had to work to supplement their family incomes, in 1860 for example, accounted for 40 percent of the 8,000 persons employed in the town's various manufacturing establishments. These kinds of conditions continued well into the 20th century.

The influx of newcomers upset some long-time New Haven residents who saw their traditional neighborhoods dotted with non-Yankee, non-Protestant, Irish, and German "foreigners." Close to 3,000 inhabitants in 1860 were foreign-born, mainly Irish

Chapel and State streets, 1907. The accoutrements of modern urban life produced a central business district cluttered with trolley tracks, water hydrants, sewer drains, fire alarm boxes, electric wires, and telephone poles. Photo by T. S. Bronson. (NHCHS)

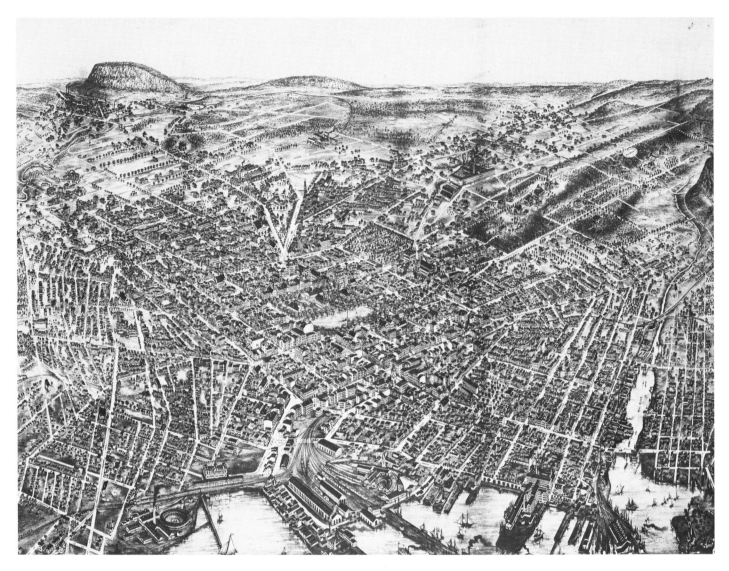

The rapid expansion of the city in the years after the Civil War is vividly depicted in this 1879 lithograph by Bailey and Hazen of Boston. The open land to the north would disappear as the century progressed. (NHCHS)

Catholics but also a sprinkling of Germans, both of Jewish and Christian religious affiliation. One reflection of the city's increasing cultural diversity was the proliferation of religious institutions; in 1855 New Haven had 27 churches and one synagogue.

Although many white European newcomers to New Haven remained in an economically precarious state for years, and were periodically subject to prejudice, their lot was considerably better than that of the Afro-Americans whose entire lives seemed to be defined by menial work, segregated housing, and their color. The city's black community, descended from slaves brought to the New Haven area during the colonial era, increased slowly between 1774 and 1850, but then, because blacks came to New Haven seeking work in the 1850s, almost doubled

by 1860. But they were not only denied skilled work in the city's burgeoning industries; virtually no black had the capital or experience necessary to open his own business or shop.

Meanwhile, New Haven's emerging needs were gradually recognized and stimulated an impulse for civic improvement. The city's principal urban services today, whether public or private, are largely a creation of the 19th century, some before and some after the Civil War, although continually modernized as technology improved. As was traditional in America, most urban services were provided by private corporations under regulation of the municipal government. Only such necessities as police and fire protection, streets, harbor facilities, and public markets were regarded as city or public responsibilities.

Top
An economic fact of life at the turn of the century: black New Haveners, like these porters in the lobby of the New Haven House Hotel, were hired for jobs from which they were not permitted to rise. (NHCHS)

Left
New Haven turned out in force to watch the Second Regiment of Connecticut Volunteers march off to the Civil War. Despite enlistment bonuses provided by the national and state governments, the economic situation became so desperate for so many local people that $200,000 was appropriated at a town meeting for the relief of draftees and their families in the summer of 1863. From the Dana Collection, NHCHS.

By 1860 New Haven was a prosperous, regionally significant community with a growing economy and population. The Civil War, begun in 1861, threatened not only the survival of the United States but also the Elm City's economic future. Manufacturers, spurred on by government contracts, swiftly converted from consumer goods to the production of war materiel, and instead of economic depression New Haven underwent boom conditions in some industries. And this, more than any other factor, is the reason why the city's population increased some 10,000 during the 1860–1870 decade.

Although war contracts buoyed the New Haven economy and Connecticut escaped the ravages of battle on its soil, the city and state paid an exceptionally heavy price in human lives: 20,000 of Connecticut's 55,000 soldiers were

wounded and 5,578 were killed. The Soldiers' and Sailors' Monument on East Rock, overlooking the city since its construction in 1886, lists 420 New Haven residents killed in the war. Relative to New Haven's population, the death and casualty rate was very high.

As some industries shifted away from prewar patterns and war contracts during the late 1860s and into the 1870s, many laborers were faced with long periods of unemployment. Yet New Haven did manage to avoid the worst effects of war's end and the national depression of 1873 and it slowly began another era of sustained economic growth between the 1870s and 1920s. This was possible because of the city's strong, diversified manufacturing industries, its direct transportation connections with New York and Boston and through them with the rest of

America, and the separate but mutually reinforcing economic activities of Yale University, private business, New Haven city government, and the federal government.

Yale University contributed immeasurably to New Haven's cultural atmosphere, preventing the city from becoming just another American factory town, and it played a vital economic role in the community as well. Between 1870 and 1900, Yale's student and faculty population grew from 819 to 2,944. Several thousand students and faculty required an incredibly wide array of services, employing a small army of local residents; in addition, many small businesses near the university emerged to attend to students' needs and whims. To provide the kind of educational quality capable of attracting students from all over the nation, Yale had become, without realizing or desiring it, one of the city's biggest businesses and has remained so in the 20th century.

Employment opportunities in transportation, manufacturing, and new industries based on electrical power also underlay continued city growth. Transportation is the spinal cord of any city, and developments in city transit both reflected and shaped New Haven's economic vitality as well as its geographical expansion. Radiating outward from Church and Chapel streets—the business and governmental centers—were city "trolleys" that reached, eventually, into every part of the city and nearby suburban villages and communities. The system had begun in 1860 when a street railway company was chartered to construct a horse-drawn carriage line between Fair Haven and Westville, with branches into other sections of New Haven. A city

council committee, created for that purpose, oversaw not only the laying of the iron track on which the coaches would run but also regulated subsequent operations of the streetcar lines. The trolley network pulled the various New Haven neighborhoods together, made the shopping district accessible to city dwellers, contributed to the growth of nearby suburban communities, and firmly established the Green in the public's mind as the psychological center as well as business and governmental center of the New Haven area. In the meantime, railroads were connecting New Haven with the rest of the United States.

In 1893 the street railways were redesigned to run by electricity. In 1893, also, the city government contracted with the company to provide electric lighting for public buildings, although most city buildings continued to use gas illumination for a decade or more. Within a few years, in 1899, the company was renamed the United Illuminating Company and became, like the Southern New England Telephone Company, another major 20th-century landowner, employer, and influence within New Haven. In the years after the Civil War, manufacturing, education, transportation, and new industries based on electricity developed or rapidly expanded and changed the physical landscape of New Haven.

Responding to the imperatives of rapid growth, city leaders began modernizing New Haven's basic urban services and the structure of municipal institutions, laying the foundations of the 20th-century city. Because the major political parties drew their mayoral candidates from the local business-entrepreneurial elite, the actions of city government in the 19th and early 20th

centuries obviously reflected its views about what the city should do. Under its leadership, the government upgraded municipal services and enhanced the quality of New Haven life for the people while simultaneously stimulating the local economy and advancing the interests of the business elites.

For a time, however, these efforts were overshadowed by an intense political struggle over the final location of Connecticut's capital. This long-simmering contest between New Haven and Hartford, the state's co-capitals, reached its bitter climax between 1867 and 1873. New Haven lost the battle and in October 1873 ceased to be the co-capital of Connecticut.

Meanwhile the city's arterial system of streets, bridges, and harbor facilities was given considerable attention, and public buildings of many kinds were being constructed east of the Green in the heart of the city, some of which would be in use well into the 20th century. After long agitation, beginning in the early 1850s, the new City Hall was authorized and opened in 1862, followed by the County Courthouse in 1874, which served a variety of important city functions. Housed on the first floor was the Police Department, which the city and state had reorganized in 1861 and placed under the charge of the six-member Board of Police Commissioners. On the second floor were the city courts, and on the third floor were the Board of Health (created in 1873) and the Board of Commissioners of the reorganized city Fire Department. A fire-alarm telegraph system, consisting of strategically placed alarm boxes, as well as a new hydrant system, was developed. Adding to the innovations was Henry S. Parmelee's

The paths of East Rock Park provided an escape from the busy streets and noisy factories of the city. T. S. Bronson snapped these girls as they relaxed from a hike on December 19, 1909. (NHCHS)

automatic sprinkler system, which was widely adopted for use within the city. And last, a new public market was completed in the 1870s on Chapel and Union streets.

The foundations of the modern public school and public park systems were also laid in this era. The city had many private schools and supported many local public schools, but it was not until 1856, when the state mandated the creation of a Board of Education, that the district schools scattered all over the city were brought under central direction. Eventually this system grew to 31 elementary schools, six middle schools, and six high schools by the 1970s.

The city began in earnest, in these years, to develop a park system for the New Haven population. By 1900 this system included the East Rock, West Rock, Edgewood, and Waterside parks; by the 1970s the municipal park system comprehended 2,500 acres of public parks within the city's 14,400 acres of land and consisted of 21 parks, 48 playgrounds, 52 tennis courts, 3 ice-skating rinks, 45 ballfields, a 15,000-seat stadium, and a Revolutionary War fort, among other things.

Yale University and New Haven are so intimately associated in the public mind that they have become almost synonymous, but six other colleges also enhance New Haven's cultural life. The city has been fortunate to be the home of Albertus Magnus College, a Catholic liberal-arts residential college for women. Established in 1925, it is the oldest institution of its kind in New England and has been operated by the Dominican Sisters since its founding. The Dominican spirit at Albertus has encouraged students to seek knowledge and understanding and to share their wisdom with others they meet.

Quinnipiac College, a private coeducational college now located in Hamden, at the foot of Sleeping Giant Mountain, was in 1929 the Connecticut College of Commerce. In 1951 it became Quinnipiac College and received authority to award the bachelor's degree. As with most state colleges,

Southern Connecticut State College began as a "normal" school for training teachers. That was in 1893. Continual growth since that time has brought about the evolution of Southern Connecticut into a multi-functional college with an enrollment of 11,500 students.

In 1920 the University of New Haven opened as New Haven YMCA college, a branch of Northeastern University. For 40 years the lack of its own facilities limited the school's growth, but with the purchase of the nucleus of its present campus in 1960, the University of New Haven began to develop into a full-scale undergraduate and graduate university. South Central Community College and the Greater New Haven State Technical College do not have as long histories as their sister schools; but each, in a relatively short time, has come to serve important educational needs in the area; South Central is a two-year college of the arts and technologies and Greater New Haven State Technical College prepares technicians to meet the changing needs of Connecticut business and industry.

Three major hospitals have developed in the New Haven area. Yale-New Haven Hospital, organized in 1826 as the General Hospital Society of Connecticut, was the first hospital in the state. Through the years it has been known as State Hospital, New Haven Hospital, Knight United States Army General Hospital, New Haven Hospital, Grace-New Haven Community Hospital, and—in 1965—Yale-New Haven Hospital. By this decade of the 20th century, it had become the largest community hospital in the state and was acknowledged as one of the 10 best in the nation.

In 1907 the Sisters of Charity of St. Elizabeth founded the hospital of St. Raphael. Originally located in a house on Chapel Street which the sisters had converted into a 12-bed hospital, St. Raphael's has grown into one of the most modern facilities in New England, especially after the opening in 1976 of the Verde Memorial Building. It has been a major teaching hospital,

offering postgraduate medical education in all major specialties.

The United States Government, in 1948, bought the former William Wirt Winchester Hospital in West Haven—a tuberculosis hospital that had been opened in 1918—and converted it into a Veterans Administration hospital. The 700-bed hospital came to perform a wide range of medical services, in particular developing epilepsy and eye research centers that are prominent referral facilities for the eastern United States. The hospital has worked closely with both Yale-New Haven and St. Raphael's in research projects in a variety of fields.

The Fourth Estate has been an important part of New Haven's history since 1755. In that year Benjamin Franklin came to New Haven to begin a newspaper, the first in Connecticut, called the *Connecticut Gazette*. Managed by a series of editors including Franklin's nephew, Benjamin Mecom, the weekly newspaper lasted for 13 years and 596 issues. The paper's assets then became the property of Samuel and Thomas Green, editors of the *Connecticut Journal and New Haven Post Boy*. The Green family controlled the journal until 1835, when Thomas G. Woodward and John B. Carrington purchased it, eventually changing its name to the *Morning Journal and Courier* and making it a daily paper.

Meanwhile in 1812, Joseph Barber began publication of the *Columbian Register*. This paper in 1875 became the *New Haven Evening Register*. By the end of the century the paper was facing financial collapse. But the newspaper's young managing editor saw hope for the *Register*, found a partner in Samuel A. York, and bought the troubled newspaper. The young editor was John Day Jackson, and he made the *Register* a success, with a circulation of more than 100,000. In 1926 Jackson bought the former *Morning Journal and Courier*, its name was changed to the *New Haven Journal-Courier* in 1906, and maintained as a separate paper from the *Register*. Both papers, known as the

Jackson Newspapers were purchased in 1986 by Ingersoll Publications who discontinued the Journal-
Courier in March 1987.

A final achievement of late 19th-
century municipal leaders was the
modernization of New Haven's city
government. From 1784 through 1897,
New Haven had both a town government and a city government. The Town
of New Haven (about eight square
miles) was bounded by Hamden, Orange, Woodbridge, the waters of the
harbor, and the Mill River. At the Town
Meeting, residents of the Town of New
Haven annually selected a Town Se-
lectman and 150 other officers to govern the entire area. Within the town
area lay the City of New Haven, which
had been granted its own city charter
by the state legislature in 1784. The
city's boundaries were the Mill River
to the east, the West River to the west,
and Mill River Meadow to the north,
and down to the waterfront. City residents elected a mayor and city council
(known officially as the Court of the
Common Council) who together had
primary jurisdiction within the City of
New Haven.

As the city grew more complex, the
exercise of public authority by town
officials within the city seemed increasingly intolerable to city officers, and a
movement began in the early 1850s to
merge the two governments. It was not
until 1897 that the consolidation of
town with city was finally effected.

After consolidation the city government assumed responsibility for all
public functions within the town; in
effect, the city absorbed the town. With
the exception of the judicial system, all
local public functions were concentrated in the municipal government; a
mayor (elected citywide), a city council
(elected representatives from each of
the wards), and many independent
boards (whose commissioners were
appointed by the mayor for fixed terms)
responsible for overseeing the city de-
partments, personnel, and the execu-
tion of most city functions.

The most significant alteration in

city government structure between the
late 19th and early 20th centuries—besides those resulting from expansion
of functions and personnel—concerned the city council. In 1877, for example, voters in the 12 wards elected
60 men (24 aldermen and 36 council-
men), who together composed the
"Court of Common Council," although
the real legislative power within the
city resided in the Board of Aldermen.
The two-house council proved to be
unwieldy after consolidation, however, and in June 1902 it was abolished.
Thereafter the Board of Aldermen became solely responsible for passage of
local ordinances and approval of the
municipal budget.

Even before consolidation, however, New Haven was geographically
expanding. Indeed, throughout the
19th century as New Haven grew, it
nurtured the development of small
population clusters on its edges, like
beads on a string, whose people were
economically dependent on the city.
New Haven had only four wards in
1853 but had 12 in 1877. During the
1890s the city seemed to be "bursting
its bounds in all directions" and three
more wards were added at the time of
the consolidation. After another major
round of population growth and land
development, the city in 1921 responded to the need for more adequate
political representation by more than
doubling the number of wards and aldermen from 15 to 33. The city tried to
cope with some of the changes by improving, modernizing, and expanding the functions of New Haven's
municipal government, but they have
only slightly modified the structure of
city government although the city has
grown and changed in ways un-
dreamed of 50 or 75 years ago.

Most of today's New Haven was
built between the 1890s and 1920s as
the city completed its transformation
into an industrial metropolis. The federal government helped with its massive contracts for guns and military
equipment for the Spanish-American
War (1898–1900), the Philippine Insur-

gency (1900–1902), and World War I (1915–1918). Workers and their families streamed into the city for war industry jobs and New Haven's population jumped upward to 162,537 by 1920. Most of the newcomers were unskilled laborers from eastern Europe and southern Italy. Under the pressure of population growth, whole new neighborhoods sprouted. Despite many outward appearances of growth and prosperity, however, the "new" New Haven looked increasingly like many another blighted factory town. Factories, tenement houses, and traffic-choked streets seemed to symbolize the city rather than the sprawling Yale University campus, the boulevard-like streets, and the tree-lined neighborhoods where the well-to-do lived. New Haven also had three large slum areas by the turn of the century, which seemed daily to grow. Most of New Haven's newcomers gravitated to these areas to live; they could afford little else

Above

Chapel Street, 1959. During the 1920s national chain stores began to take the place of locally owned businesses on Chapel Street. The older New Haven stores found it hard to compete with the cheaper prices offered at the new outlets. From the Dana Collection, NHCHS.

Right

The ease of commuting by automobile enabled those who could afford it to escape the city and move to a quieter, less crowded suburb. The Wilson family and their canine companion posed for the camera of William Starr Horton near their home in Woodbridge circa 1910. (NHCHS)

when they arrived.

Besides new buildings, outer neighborhoods, and inner slums, the face of New Haven changed in other ways characteristic of the 20th century. Among the most visible were the growing number of cars and trucks on the streets and the new kinds of retail stores all over the city. During the 1920s the city underwent a commercial revolution with the opening of national outlets. Indeed, the city seemed to be deluged with national chain stores. Many local retail businesses, unable to compete, were in decline, and this hastened the appearance of blight in the downtown business district. This was only a glimpse, however, of what was to happen to city businesses of all kinds with the advent, in the 1950s, of national chain-owned shopping centers in nearby suburban towns.

Of all the changes, however, the greatest was the growth of New Haven's suburbs as middle- and upper-income families moved out of the city. Contemporaries noticed this population drift but did not realize its real implications. By 1920 New Haven had become a metropolis—the central city of a sprawling metropolitan area. Circling the city, but beyond its legal boundaries, were the adjacent towns whose growth was closely linked to that of New Haven. The United States Census in 1920 regarded these communities as integral parts of the New Haven Metropolitan District. Within New Haven's metropolitan district, there were more than 205,000 people, of whom some 162,537 lived in the central city. By 1930 the district total had risen to 233,656, but New Haven's population remained stationary. Even during subsequent economically depressed years, the suburbs continued to grow while New Haven marked time and by the 1950s actually began to lose pop-

NEW HAVEN METROPOLITAN AREA

	City of New Haven	Greater New Haven* (New Haven and 10 Suburban Towns)	Area Towns (Excluding New Haven)
1850	20,345		
1860	40,000	55,400	15,400
1870	50,840	69,051	18,175
1880	62,882	82,771	19,889
1890	86,045	102,075	16,030
1900	108,000	133,689	25,689
1910	133,605	145,130	11,525
1920	162,537	205,371	42,834
1930	162,655	233,656	71,001
1940	160,605	246,436	85,831
1950**	164,443	273,045	108,602
1960	152,048	342,296	190,248
1970	137,707	355,538	217,831
1980	125,787	338,200	212,413

*As defined by the United States Census Department, the Standard Metropolitan Statistical Area of New Haven (or Greater New Haven Area) consists of the following 11 communities: New Haven, Bethany, Branford, East Haven, Guilford, Hamden, North Branford, North Haven, Orange, Woodbridge, and West Haven.

**The first Census that counted Yale University students. Without Yale students in 1950, New Haven's population would have been 155,924. Without Yale students in 1960, New Haven's population would have been 144,255.

ulation (see chart).

Many northeastern and midwestern cities had experienced, or were undergoing, the same population exodus, but friendly state legislatures allowed them to absorb their suburbs through wholesale consolidation of adjacent towns and "annexation" of unincorporated population clusters on their outskirts. New Haven's neighboring communities had been separate towns, however, since the colonial period and jealously guarded their identities. The process of urban-suburban growth in southern Connecticut therefore did not result in the evolution of a single very large city. Instead, New Haven was destined to remain a small-to-medium-sized city surrounded by a ring of prosperous middle-income, even wealthy communities.

New Haven's 20th-century "character" is less a product of the city's past history and culture than its unique mixture of peoples. It is a city of foreign immigrants and American-born migrants. The ultimate achievement of 20th-century New Haven may be the

gradual, and largely peaceful, absorption of many different kinds of people into the life of the city and metropolitan area. Italians are, and have been, the largest ethnic or nationality group within the city and the greater New Haven area for most of the century, but there have also been significant numbers of Armenians, Chinese, Greeks, Irish, Lithuanians, Poles, Romanians, Russians, and Ukrainians, among others, who influenced the area's development. Also there have been migrants to New Haven from other parts of the country, including native-born white Americans of every conceivable background, black Americans from the South, and American citizens from Puerto Rico. Each group brought to New Haven its own cultural style and religious perspective.

Since the turn of the century, then, New Haven has been a multiethnic, multicultural, multiracial city subdivided into white Gentile groups, blacks and other nonwhites, and Jews. As early as 1910 one-third of the 133,000 people were foreign-born immigrants

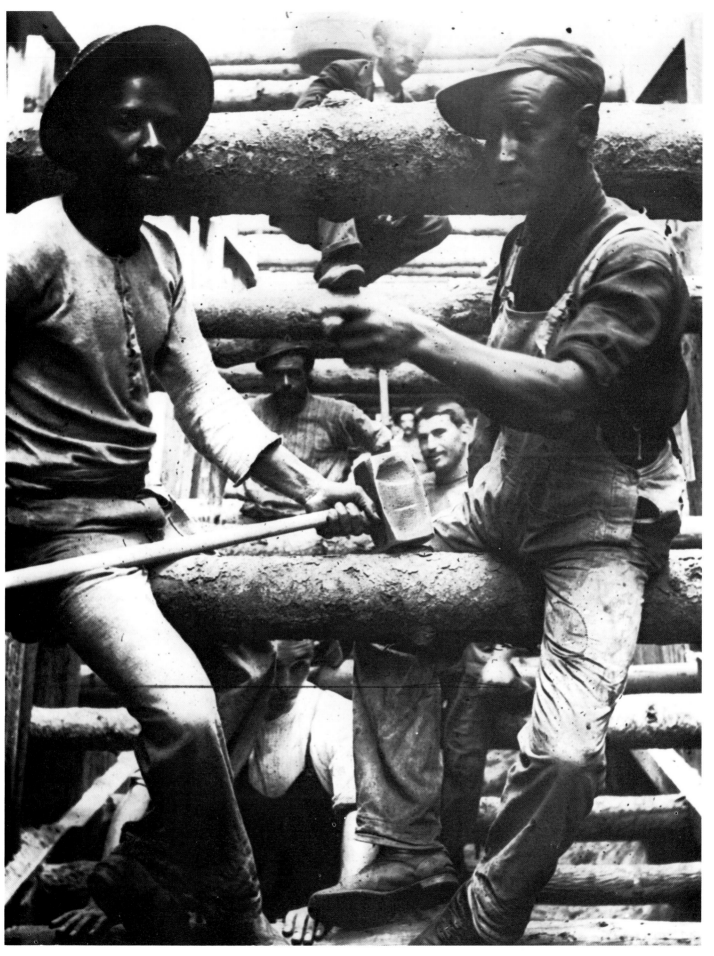

(so-called first generation Americans) and another third (the second generation) had at least one immigrant parent.

The earlier Irish and German immigrants of the 1830s, 1840s, and 1850s located in the Hill section off Congress Avenue where the cheapest housing could be found, then moved all over the city as their incomes improved. During the 1880s and 1890s northern Italians moved into the Hill section of Oak Street, while southern Italian immigrants gravitated to the Wooster Square area, nearer the factories where most worked. Eastern Europeans, mainly Jews from Russia, lived in the northwestern periphery of the Hill, along Oak Street, while Poles were situated to the northeast of the Green.

Generally newcomers arrived at the center of the city, closest to the Green, in the poorest and oldest areas, and were gradually absorbed into the city's economy and life. Over time they became upwardly mobile, and the second generation moved outward into the next ring or area of the city, usually nearer the city's edges. By the 1950s and 1960s their children, the third generation, moved into New Haven's suburbs.

The only exception to this pattern of economic and geographic mobility applied to blacks. Afro-Americans lived in the Oak Street area, among other places, around the turn of the century, but most were crowded out and found their way, increasingly, to the 20-block Dixwell Avenue area, named after the avenue that bisects it, northeast of the Green. Over the course of time, few blacks have been able, easily, to move elsewhere in the city, especially into neighborhoods clearly dominated by one or another white ethnic group, or to the suburbs.

The grandparents and parents of many of New Haven's suburban dwellers originally lived and raised their families in these and similar city areas. In return for their cheap labor, the city's industries and public services, such as schools, enabled many of them to move up, and in time some were able to move out to the suburbs. For those with only meager resources—money, education, or work skills—mobility was more likely in New Haven before the 1950s than after, however, because so many of the city's major manufacturing industries left during the 1950s. For skilled workers and professionals, New Haven offered greater opportunities much more quickly. Although very few in the first generation were professionals such as doctors, lawyers, teachers, newspaper editors, and clergymen, there were more in the second generation and still more in the third.

Neither the Great Depression of the 1930s nor World War II had as great an impact upon New Haven's 20th-century development as the postwar flight of well-to-do whites to nearby suburbs and the in-migration of disadvantaged blacks and Hispanics. Between 1945 and 1960 New Haven underwent an economic and social transformation rivaling that of 1860–1920.

The war's end released almost two decades of pent-up energies, desires, and consumer purchasing power. A middle class, enlarged and made prosperous by the war, abandoned the cities all over the Northeast and Midwest in search of larger homes, better schools, higher status, and less crowded living conditions in the suburbs. These outlying communities, reachable only by car, seemed to explode with popu-

An increasing number of New Haven's citizens migrated to the suburbs after the Second World War. The result was a steady decline in sales for merchants in the downtown area, including the proprietor of this Edgewood Avenue grocery store, who was photographed in March of 1953 by T. S. Bronson. (NHCHS)

Houses like this one on Academy Street have been saved from total decay thanks to the Wooster Square Restoration Project sponsored by the New Haven Redevelopment Agency. Courtesy, New Haven Redevelopment Agency.

lation, single-family dwellings, and shopping facilities, while New Haven continued to decline.

As the well-off left, business and industry followed, and New Haven ceased to be the vital center of the metropolitan area for retail shopping. Since more than half of the stores in the Church Street area had been built before 1885, New Haven's merchants found it extremely difficult to compete with new stores located in more modern shopping centers with convenient free parking.

To add to the decline, between 1947 and 1980, manufacturing jobs were reduced in New Haven from 34,500 to 14,500, while in the same years suburban jobs, not necessarily all manufacturing positions of course, increased from 19,400 to 101,000. This signaled yet another profound alteration within the greater New Haven area. By the early 1960s the suburban towns had become, collectively, *the* job creators in the metropolitan area.

Because city leaders did not under-

stand the historical forces reshaping Greater New Haven, the municipal government from the 1920s through the early 1950s failed to do anything about the city's deterioration. Finally, under the aggressive leadership of Mayor Richard C. Lee, the city did try to arrest the precipitous decline of New Haven. From 1954, through eight mayoral terms, Lee carried out an unprecedented, large-scale program of urban renewal and became nationally famous. Though unable to reverse the trend, Lee's attempt at redevelopment transformed, once again, the landscape of New Haven.

The keystone of this program was rebuilding the downtown area around Church Street to bring suburban shoppers back to New Haven. Everything hinged upon easy access to the city by private cars. Once the state highway department was persuaded to build a six-lane highway link—the Oak Street Connector—from the Connecticut Turnpike into the heart of the city, all the pieces of the intricate plan fell into

place. Grant money flowed in from federal, state, and private sources. Clearance of the city's worst slum, Oak Street, began in 1957. In its place rose new luxury housing, office buildings, shopping malls, medical buildings—all flanking a new six-lane Oak Street Connector.

Nearby in the Church Street Project, new Macy's and Malley's department stores and Chapel Square Mall, Park Plaza Hotel, office towers, and 1500 structured parking spaces were erected. Retail sales swung upward for the first time in decades. Middle-class families moved into the new housing. Investment flowed anew into the city's core. New Haven appeared reborn.

Spurred by this success, the program expanded into the residential areas. The country's first residential rehabilitation project, Wooster Square, employed a combination of clearance and widespread rehabilitation to demonstrate that a decaying neighborhood could indeed be renewed.

Although the renewal program eventually grew to cover a full third of the city's land area and produced new housing, schools, parks, fire stations, factories, and other facilities, it could not entirely stem the exodus of middle-class families to suburbia, nor reverse the trend of shopping at numerous new suburban malls. Nor could it prevent the brief but stunning riots of 1967 and 1968 in several inner-city areas.

By the end of Mayor Lee's last term in 1969, growing dissatisfaction with clearance in general, and several proposed projects in particular, coupled with massive reductions in federal funding, led to a sharp decline in New Haven's renewal activities.

The ambitious renewal program is still debated as a boon or bane upon the cityscape. What the future of New Haven may be is uncertain. But the metropolitan area which New Haven helped create is a vibrant, prosperous community, and all acknowledge that without a thriving city at the center, the future would be bleak for all.

The Second Empire Gamble-Desmond Building was demolished along with the Glebe Building and the Edward Malley stores to make way for the Chapel Square Mall. The mall was one of the many projects undertaken to restore economic viability to downtown New Haven during the administration of Mayor Richard C. Lee. Photo of Gamble-Desmond Building by Willis N. Butricks, NHCHS. Chapel Square Mall photo courtesy, New Haven Redevelopment Agency.

Chapter IV

NEW HAVEN AND THE SEA

by Gaddis Smith

The name that the original settlers gave to their colony was both a spiritual metaphor and a literal maritime description: New Haven, the new refuge, the new harbor. From the first settlement of 1638 until the mid-19th century, the sea was New Haven's principal means of trade and travel and a significant provider of jobs and profit. Energy, in the broadest sense, is the key to understanding New Haven's maritime history. Colonial New Haven produced exportable energy in the form of food and animals. Hundreds of small New Haven sailing vessels carried the food to the sugar islands of the West Indies in return for molasses, rum, and bills of exchange with which to purchase manufactured goods imported via Boston or New York from Europe. With the rise of manufacturing in New Haven in the 19th century, the importation of energy in the form of coal replaced the export of food as the dominant maritime activity. The age of coal gave way in the 1940s to the age of petroleum when nearly all the energy that generated the city's electricity, warmed its buildings, and powered its vehicles, arrived by sea. The three ages of New Haven's relationship to the sea—food, coal, and petroleum—illustrate the point that the history of what people do on land explains their uses of the sea.

New Haven's maritime history also illustrates the controlling influence of geography. The leaders of the infant colony were men of high commercial ambition. They dreamed of making New Haven a center of transatlantic trade and themselves rich. They invested too much in one basket: the ill-fated "Phantom Ship" of 1646 was lost with all hands on a voyage to England and afterward celebrated in legend and poem. The incident symbolizes maritime New Haven's habit, persisting to the present, of embracing great expectations only to see them founder on the rocks of geographical reality. The harbor, good by local standards, was not big or deep enough to sustain the trade of a world port, especially given the proximity of Boston and New York. But dreamers should not be condemned if in their more practical moments they make good use, as did the maritime leaders of New Haven, of resources at hand.

New Haven harbor is a broad indentation on Long Island Sound, 75 miles from Manhattan and the same distance from the open Atlantic off Block Island. Protected by three outlying breakwaters since the late 19th century, the outer harbor is four miles wide. The inner harbor, four miles inland at the confluence of the Mill and Quinnipiac Rivers, is naturally shallow and less than a quarter mile wide. Shallowness and silting were problems

The cargo arriving on this three-masted bark was loaded directly onto freight cars of the New York, New Haven and Hartford Railroad in the late 19th century. (NHCHS)

The brig Favorite, *shown here entering New Haven Harbor circa 1865, was employed in the West Indies trade. Crossing the Gulf Stream was hazardous: a severe storm could force a captain to throw his cargo of livestock overboard in order to save the vessel.* (NHCHS)

from the first years of the colony. This circumstance led immediately to improvements upon nature: wharves into deeper water, landfilling of tidal flats and creeks, and eventual dredging. The crowning improvement was Long Wharf which, by the early 19th century, extended more than half a mile into deep water and supported dozens of shops, taverns, warehouses, and offices on its broad back.

After the loss of the Phantom Ship, New Haven's merchants and seafarers concentrated on serving the needs of the colony's agricultural hinterland. Farmers brought in their corn, wheat, rye, peas, pork, beef, cattle, horses, staves, and lumber. Some of this produce was carried to small ports along the Connecticut shore, some to Boston, and some to New York. But the greatest part went to the West Indies to feed the black slaves who were growing sugar, the most valuable commodity in the international trade of the 17th and 18th centuries. New Haven vessels brought back sugar in refined form or as molasses and extraordinary quantities of rum, together with salt (an essential preservative before the introduction of refrigeration), a little fruit, a little coffee, and occasionally a black slave (usually called a "servant"). The West Indies trade produced a credit balance for New Haven and for all the mainland communities involved in it. New Haven merchants used the

credit balances, expressed in documents called bills of exchange, to buy from abroad what the colonists could not make at home: fine furniture and clothing, tools and cutlery, medicines, books, and hundreds of other items.[1] These imports were exchanged in turn to the farmers for the products of the land, the food energy to sustain the slaves who grew the sugar. And thus the cycle continued.

Ocean transportation in the age of sail was very labor-intensive. About one quarter of those who lived in the town of New Haven in the colonial period worked at occupations directly connected with the sea and shipping: captains and seamen, shipwrights and ropemakers, riggers and coopers, sellers of all that a vessel could require, and merchants who controlled the trade and usually owned the ships.[2] The vessels, often locally built, were predominantly sloops, i.e., single-masted with a large gaff-rigged mainsail, several jibs leading to a long bowsprit, and often a square topsail. They seldom exceeded 60 feet in length or 50 tons of cargo capacity. They were sailed typically by a captain, mate, two to four seamen, and a cabin boy who was quite often a black. Only toward the end of the 18th century did larger vessels— two-masted brigs and schooners and three-masted ships—appear regularly in New Haven.

The West Indies trade was filled

Crewmen found ingenious ways to pass the long hours at sea. The Minerva Wedmore *was immortalized on a breadboard by the ship's cook in the 1870s. (NHCHS)*

ith dangers from nature and man. olonial newspapers offer an unbroken litany of disasters: men and cargo ashed overboard, vessels aground on ncharted reefs or engulfed by hurricanes, men dead of fever, vessels taken y privateers or confiscated because ne nation or another in an age of almost perpetual war had suddenly hanged the rules. The trade was also ubject to frustrating delays and uncertainty. First, the New Haven merchants had to collect a cargo by dvertising in the weekly paper. The oyage south to Barbados, for example, could last from two weeks to well ver a month. The vessel had to cross he Gulf Stream with its ferocious qualls and steep seas. Cargoes of orses and cattle, in which New Haven pecialized, were particularly hazardus on the topheavy sloops. Assuming safe arrival in the West Indies, the aptain might find the local market lutted. He would then proceed from ne island to another in search of an cceptable price. Sometimes a vessel ould remain in one place for months aiting for buyers or gathering a omebound cargo. Repairs to the vessel or the need to replace crew members who had deserted, died, or been ospitalized, often led to further delay. he result was that few vessels could omplete more than two round-trip oyages in a year.

The war of the American Revolu-

tion temporarily destroyed New Haven's commerce, but peace brought prosperity. Many historians once accepted the Federalist view that the years between the Revolution and the formation of the new government under the Constitution were a time of extreme economic stagnation; New Haven's condition contradicts this view. Well before the preliminary peace of 1781, New Haven vessels had resumed active trade with the West Indies. Some, it is true, were captured by British privateers, but trade and profits mounted. Newspaper advertisements tell the story. The schooner *Polly* will exchange salt, blubber, and blubber oil for "Country Produce." H. Sabin, Jr., has "West India rum or molasses given in exchange for Indian Corn."

For two heady decades New Haven appeared to have broken out of the confines of local and West Indies trade into the circle of world commerce. A steady trade developed with Ireland, carrying flaxseed for the Irish linen industry, thence to England, returning to New Haven with manufactured goods.[3] Other vessels traded directly with France, Spain, and the Canary Islands, bringing back wine, the favored drink of the newly prosperous. In 1793 war broke out between England and France and continued with only brief interruption until 1815. As in colonial times, war meant huge risks and profits. New Haveners found their share

When he was 30 years of age, Daniel Greene took command of the ship Neptune, *owned by Ebenezer Townsend of New Haven, and sailed for China. The* Neptune *circumnavigated the globe on a three-year cruise and netted profits of one quarter of a million dollars. (NHCHS)*

of both.

The profits of wartime trade were partially reinvested in New Haven's most romantic maritime venture: the dispatch of a fleet of large vessels used in the killing of fur seals in the far South Atlantic, thence with the furs to China, and home around the globe to New Haven with tea, fine fabrics, and china- ware. The first and largest of this fleet was the ship *Neptune* of 360 tons and 20 guns. She sailed in 1796, gathered furs, stopped at the Hawaiian Islands, proceeded to China, and returned to New Haven in 1799 with a cargo of tea, cloth, and tableware on which a duty of $75,000 was paid. Fewer than 20 ves- sels in all comprised the China fleet and they produced a concentrated burst of maritime prosperity never to be re- peated in the city's history.[4]

Three things destroyed New Ha- ven's particular version of the China trade: the sealers, without a modern conservationist ethic, decimated the seals; the market in China rapidly grew saturated and the price of even scarce skins dropped; and President Thomas Jefferson's embargo of 1807 banned all American foreign trade.

The embargo, vociferously op- posed by New Haven's maritime lead- ership, was Jefferson's response to the violation by both Britain and France of American neutral rights. The most se- rious violation was the British practice of impressment, the virtual kidnap- ping of American seamen on the high seas in order to fill the depleted ranks on British warships. The embargo lasted two years, but neither it nor less strin- gent measures of economic warfare adopted in the administration of James Madison, worked. In June 1812 a sharply divided Congress voted for war. The representatives of maritime interests were opposed.

The War of 1812 marked a turning point in the economic history of New Haven. After the war the West Indies trade resumed on a diminished and dwindling scale. The China trade did not revive; other direct foreign trade virtually disappeared. A major factor

was the rise of the New York port to national preeminence. New Haven and the neighboring towns were in the midst of the transformation from a pri- marily agricultural to a primarily in- dustrial economy which reversed the flow of energy through the harbor. Food now began to be imported, es- pecially grain and flour from new lands in the West tapped by the Erie Canal. The growing urban-industrial popula- tion also needed lumber for homes, firewood for fuel, and from the 1840s on, coal—thousands and thousands of schooners full of coal via the Delaware River and Norfolk, Virginia.

The coal came for the railroads which radiated like spokes from New Haven; it came for the swift sidewheel passenger steamers which replaced the packet sloops on the shuttle to New York; above all it came for the station- ary steam engines which powered the machines that fashioned the guns, clocks, hardware, and carriages for which New Haven was becoming fa- mous. New Haven harbor, during the 19th-century industrial revolution, was not romantic but it was busy. The grimy and deep-draft schooners, bear- ing such prosaic names as *Reading Rail- road No. 43*, carried 20 times the weight of cargo of the *Sallys* and *Pollys*, typical sloops of the previous century. The demand for coal even brought a minor revival of direct foreign trade as large foreign square-riggers brought coal quite literally from Newcastle. Other large sailing ships brought iron from En- gland and cotton rags from Alexandria, Egypt, for New Haven's growing paper industry.

The age of coal and railroads caused the tonnage of cargo entering New Haven to double and redouble, but it doomed to failure another grand New Haven dream—that of the Farmington Canal, a project which was intended to do for New Haven what the Erie Canal had done for New York. The idea, in its full glory, called for con- nections all the way to the St. Lawrence River, thus tying New Haven to all of New England and eastern Canada. The

first boats traveled from New Haven to Farmington in 1828, just before winter ice closed navigation. By 1839, navigation had been opened from New Haven to Northampton, Massachusetts. The New Haven Packet Boat Company offered daily departures on a 24-hour trip to Northampton. The ticket on one of the company's three canalboats—*Doe*, *Hart*, and *Fawn*—cost $3.75. But the canal project lost money from the start because of low traffic from a declining farming hinterland, prolonged shutdowns because of collapsed banks, and finally, the competition of railroads. In 1847 the Farmington Canal ceased operation and was succeeded by a railroad using the canal's right of way (see Osterweis, pp. 244–49).

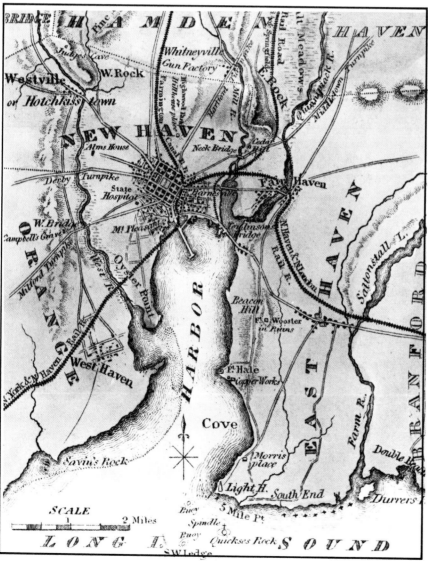

Even the settlers of the 17th century had fretted over the shallow harbor. The new activity and the larger vessels made the situation intolerable. The erection of a modern lighthouse in 1846—the same that survives today as a historical monument in Lighthouse Park—and the blasting of some underwater rocks in 1852 were useful, but still the harbor channel had a controlling depth of less than 15 feet and shipping was often damaged by storm waves from the south which surged unimpeded from the Sound to the head of the harbor. Major improvements came after the Civil War. They represented the response of Congress to the successful lobbying of the New Haven Chamber of Commerce and of one man in particular: Captain Charles Hervey Townshend.

Townshend, who rose from green hand on a West Indies brig to command of one of the largest Atlantic steamers under the American flag, might well be called the father of the modern harbor. After retiring from the sea he devoted himself to securing deeper channels and, above all, the three breakwaters—East (3,450 feet long), Middle or Luddington Rock (4,450 feet), and West (3,450 feet)—con-

68

structed between 1880 and 1915. The breakwaters not only protect the inner harbor but also provide a convenient refuge for passing craft. Today they create a vast expanse of smooth water for recreational sailing, something not anticipated by Townshend. Channel dredging under the direction of the Army Corps of Engineers began on a large scale at the end of the 19th century and is continuing.

The age of coal and steam brought a revival to shipbuilding in New Haven. In the colonial period, shipyards were small, temporary, and scattered around the harbor's edge, but by 1811, ships could be built cheaper in neighboring towns. The new industrial age, however, returned a temporary advantage to the big city. Pook's shipyard on the east shore near the mouth of the Quinnipiac, for example, launched the steamship *Admiral* in 1863, 220 feet long and hailed as the largest vessel ever built in Connecticut. A similar ship, *Captain*, followed in 1864. The climax of large shipbuilding came between 1880 and 1893 when the Gesner and Mar shipyard in West Haven, opposite City Point, launched 13 magnificent three- and four-masted schooners for coal trade. Ironically, fully laden,

they drew too much water to bring coal to New Haven where the channel had not yet been dredged to sufficient depth.

Both a cause and result of New Haven's ever-closer economic ties with New York was the early inauguration and maintenance for more than a century of passenger and freight steamboat service to the metropolis. Steamboats churned back and forth the year round except during severe cold spells when New Haven harbor was choked with ice. The early decades were marked by cutthroat competition and fluctuating fares as Commodore Cornelius Vanderbilt fought it out with rivals. The fare, usually $3 round trip, dropped to 50 cents and lower. The trip took from six to eight hours, depending on tide and weather, and was generally smooth and comfortable since the waves on Long Island Sound are rarely high enough to cause seasickness for those traveling on large craft. The vessels were well heated, served food and drink, and provided private staterooms for those who wished to pay extra. Steamboat accidents, like airline mishaps today, were rare but spectacular. Everyone could retell the story of the *Lexington*, which, in 1840,

burned near Stratford Shoal, south of Bridgeport, with the loss of 200 lives. But the New Haven boats were remarkably free of serious trouble. Now and then there was a collision with some hapless schooner in the fog or a grounding in the narrow passages and swirling riptides of the East River.

The *Richard Peck* was the most famous vessel to serve New Haven. Named for a mid-19th-century captain, she sailed almost every day for 29 years between New York and New Haven with an occasional weekend excursion. When New England Steamship, the parent company, ended New Haven service in 1920, the *Peck* was transferred to the New London run. In 1941 she went to war, sailing to Argentia, Newfoundland, to serve as a dormitory for American servicemen. After the war she returned to civilian work on the Chesapeake and was finally retired in 1953 at the age of 62.

In colonial and early national times, many of the officers and crew on vessels engaged in the city's trade were New Haveners. The Trowbridge family, for example, provided dozens of merchants and ship captains throughout much of the 18th and 19th centuries. Sometimes two or three Trowbridge captains would be listed as arriving or departing with their sloops or schooners in a single week. Steamboat officers and owners came from well-known families—Trowbridge, Townshend, Peck, and Hardy. Seamen, often homeless, transient, and semiliterate, are difficult to find or describe as individuals. City directories list ever fewer mariners or seamen as the 20th century approaches, but directories listed only those with established addresses. One important New Haven philanthropy, the Woman's Seamen's Friend Society, established in 1859 but with antecedents going back to 1812, was devoted to providing spiritual and material assistance to seamen in distress. The Society maintained a seamen's home until 1971.

At the turn of the 20th century the activities of New Haven harbor fell into three main categories: the delivery of coal in ever greater amounts, recreation, and the cultivation of oysters. Local water had never, compared to those farther east, been productive enough to sustain a large permanent fishing industry. But the oyster was another matter. A combination of natural advantages and entrepreneurial skill made New Haven the oyster capital of the nation in the 19th century. The industry, although much diminished, remains today. The hunt for the natural oyster was replaced in the mid-19th century by regulated oyster farming. Hundreds of workers, mostly women, stood all day at long counters, shucking the oysters which were canned, iced, and shipped all over the nation. In recent decades the New Haven oyster industry has suffered a succession of blows. Storms have covered the beds with silt; the Mill River and Quinnipiac River are badly polluted; the beds in cleaner water have been attacked by hordes of starfish. New Haven's seed oysters survive under constant care, but the water in which they grow is too polluted to permit direct harvesting for human consumption. They are dredged up when nearly mature and carried to cleaner waters off eastern Long Island where they are replanted for a period of cleansing and further growth.

Americans had little time or money for organized recreation, on water or land, until the mid-19th century. Waterborne recreation in New Haven follows the national pattern. Steamboat excursions and waterside hotels and restaurants appear in the 1840s. Rowing for exercise and yacht cruising and racing appear in the harbor after the Civil War. The New Haven Yacht Club, founded in 1881, prospered for half a century. Each summer in the early 20th century the elite cruising fleet of the New York Yacht Club stopped in New Haven on its way east. The 218-foot steam barque of the Crown Prince of Sweden paid a visit one gala day in June 1926. Then came three blows— the economic depression of the 1930s, the great hurricane of 1938, and World War II. When all three had passed, the New Haven Yacht Club was out of existence and remained so for a quarter century. In 1967, however, the club was revived and emphasized that membership was open to everyone interested

in sailing (no motorboats), volunteer work by members, and informality rather than brass-button pomp. The club soon acquired property in Morris Cove near its former site and by 1970 was running dozens of sailboat races in the harbor every season.

Several other institutions, born in the 1970s, enhanced the harbor as a recreational facility. Nonprofit Schooner, Inc., inspired by the success of the Hudson River sloop *Clearwater,* operated a program of environmental and maritime education featuring day trips and cruises on the large sailing vessels *Trade Wind* and *J. N. Carter.* At the same time, a group of investors estab-

lished the Long Wharf Steamship Company to operate a powered cruise vessel, *Liberty Belle,* with a capacity of 200 passengers. Thousands of New Haveners sailed on these vessels and learned firsthand that New Haven was a seaport.

The new noncommercial uses of New Haven harbor coincided with the third age of energy—the age of petroleum. After World War II petroleum rapidly replaced coal as New Haven's power source. The ponderous coal-handling facilities disappeared around the harbor and were replaced by tank farms and pipelines. The Connecticut Coke Company, last major user of coal

The New Haven Yacht Club's boathouse stood at the end of a long dock near Tomlinson's Bridge. The area was eventually filled in to create Waterside Park. (NHCHS)

at its coke manufacturing plant on the east shore, discontinued operations in 1968. The new generating plant of the United Illuminating Company, burning oil, was erected on the site.

The age of petroleum was accompanied by major alterations and improvements in the harbor. The driving force was businessman Arthur H. Gosselin, whose persistence resulted in a major deepening and broadening of the channel immediately after World War II. The dredged material was pumped ashore to create new land where the Connecticut Turnpike now skirts the harbor. The Gosselin enterprise, as it deserves to be called, completed the long transformation of the shape of the harbor which began when the first settlers dumped refuse in a tidal creek. By the 1950s the west shoreline of the harbor was a half to a full mile farther east than it had been originally.

A few New Haveners had been crying out against pollution for decades. A speaker before the Lions Club in 1935 deplored the way the Mill and Quinnipiac rivers had become obnoxious and poisoned through the slothfulness of a careless people. Such cries had little impact until the 1960s and 1970s when a combination of state and federal laws and widespread public concern began slowly but perceptibly to reverse the long process of environmental degradation. A new sewage treatment plant was constructed and older ones were improved. Industrial discharges into the harbor were curtailed by law.

As the last fifth of the 20th century began, the importation of energy in the form of oil remained overwhelmingly the most important activity of maritime New Haven. Petroleum accounted for 90 percent of all imports. The rest consisted of lumber, some steel, and chemicals. The only significant export was an end product of the age of petroleum: metal scrap, primarily from dead automobiles. The scrap, collected and processed by the Schiavone Company, was loaded by electromagnetic cranes at the New Haven Terminal into freighters headed for the steel mills of Japan, Taiwan, and Hong Kong.

The nation's and New Haven's increasing dependence on foreign oil in the 1970s brought an unprecedented number of foreign vessels into port, surpassing the coal trade from Newcastle a century before. Oil from domestic American ports was carried, as the law required, in American vessels. The oil from the Caribbean and the Middle East came in vessels, perhaps owned by American oil companies, but flying flags of Panama, Liberia, and Greece.

Let us close with a word picture of New Haven harbor on a summer day toward the end of the 20th century. In deep water several miles beyond the breakwaters, a deeply laden tanker awaits high tide and a tugboat escort before proceeding cautiously up channel to a terminal. Meanwhile a tug and gasoline barge from a New Jersey refinery, drawing less water, come boldly on. Near the breakwaters a weather-beaten oyster boat steams slowly back and forth dragging up starfish with giant string mops. A lobsterman hauls his pots from the rocky bottom off Morgan Point. At Lighthouse Point, families sun on the beach and swim in the gentle lapping waves. Recreational fishermen in small outboards drift and cast for bluefish. The multicolored sails

of windsurfers dart by. At City Point, the ketch *J. N. Carter,* with a group of high-school students aboard, prepares for a day of studying the biology of the harbor. At New Haven Terminal, a freighter with an American name, a Liberian flag, German officers, and a Spanish crew, is delivering steel from Sweden and will soon load scrap for Japan. Another freighter unloads lumber from British Columbia.

At the Chamber of Commerce that day, the Port Development Commission holds its monthly meeting. The group reviews the latest survey of the harbor, worries over the use of scarce waterfront land for nonmaritime purposes, hears that the oysters are doing well, laments that the city is unable for economic reasons to keep the fireboat *Sally Lee* in commission, and notes that, although an age of coal may be returning, the harbor no longer has coal-handling facilities. Some voices urge a campaign to expand the port, erect container-handling facilities, create a "free port," and compete with New York. It is a familiar story: the daily reality of a busy, middle-size port, and the breathless expectations of something more.

The lumber schooner New Era *gets an assist from tugboat* James H. Hogan *in this photograph by T. S. Bronson taken circa 1900. (NHCHS)*

Chapter V

NEW HAVEN INDUSTRY: A RETROSPECTIVE VIEW

by Louis I. Kuslan

The Sargent hardware factory hums with activity in this 19th-century watercolor. Opened in 1864 on Water Street, the business continues to prosper at its current location in the Long Wharf Industrial Park. Courtesy, Sargent and Company.

Why did New Haven rise to manufacturing prominence in the middle of the 19th century? New Haven was surely not blessed with natural resources, but it was blessed with citizens whose ingenuity, independence, mechanical craftsmanship, and work habits were precisely right for the newly emerging national economy.

In the 18th century the British had tried to restrict the colonies to the role of suppliers of raw materials, and banned colonial manufacturing, but the colonists easily evaded these restrictions. The result of their home-developed industry was "A huge fund of mechanical skill and aptitude ready . . . to turn to any pursuit which would make it easier to earn a living."[1]

Nearly a hundred years before the British attempted to eliminate colonial manufacturing, John Winthrop, Jr., at the invitation of the New Haven Colony established an iron forge and foundry in 1655 which refined iron from bog-iron ore dug in North Haven. Winthrop's forge operated more or less successfully until 1679. Even earlier, a water-powered gristmill supplied colonists with flour. In 1730, a water-powered sawmill was at work in Hamden. It was converted into a gristmill in 1786 and later rebult as a distillery.

With the exception of the gristmill and iron forge, the first industrial establishment in New Haven seems to

have been Abel Parmalee's bell foundry of 1736, perhaps the first in the colonies. In 1769 Abel Buell of Killingworth, an eccentric genius, successfully petitioned the Assembly to support his proposed type foundry which, however, may never have been built. In 1785, Buell was part of the group that established a mint on Water Street to produce small coins, then in short supply. Buell had perfected a machine which, within two years, minted 29,-000 pounds of copper coins. In 1787 he and a partner built a new mint on East Water Street to produce coins for the federal government.

On a trip to England to buy copper for this mint, Buell visited a number of factories that wove cotton cloth. He persuaded William McIntosh, a skilled weaver and mechanic, to migrate to New Haven where the pair built a cotton mill in Westville, operated by water power. This venture lasted just a few years.

New Haven's fame as a hardware and clock manufacturing city could not have been predicted from this history and from the handful of local artisans who fabricated and sold hardware and clocks. Isaac Doolittle, who had constructed and operated two powder mills in Westville during the Revolutionary War, made and sold brass clocks in his Chapel Street shop. Nathaniel Jocelyn, father of the painter

Nathaniel S. Jocelyn, also made brass clocks for the few who could afford them. Most New Haveners, however, were unable to buy clocks until the cheap mass-produced clocks of the 1840s were available. Precision navigational and surveying instruments, telescopes, lenses, and eyeglasses were made and sold by Jonathan Fenton as early as 1790.

In 1818, New Haven manufactories included:[2]

- 1 hat factory
- 1 nail factory
- 1 powder mill
- 2 cotton mills
- 2 paper mills
- 17 boot and shoe establishments (cobbler's shops)
- 8 chaise and wagon makers

With the emergence of the "chaise and wagon makers," the direction of New Haven manufacturing becomes clearer—from agriculture to industry to meet the new needs of a growing population. The New Haven region remained heavily agricultural, however, for most of the 19th century, even after more than half of the state's population had moved to its cities and towns by the end of the Civil War. New Haven, with its railroads and shipping, became an important market and shipping center for farm produce and industrial goods.

Instead of leather (five large tanneries were active as late as 1840), beeswax, and cordage, the principal materials shipped were "carriages, springs, clocks, boots and shoes, locks, hardware," all manufactured in or near the city or in the state. In 1860 the 216 manufactories in New Haven employed some 4,900 men and 3,100 women, of whom a quarter, predominantly men, were making carriages

and carriage accessories.

These were the industries in 1872, as listed by a local directory:[3]

Belts	1	Builder's iron	1
Brushes	1	Machine tools	5
Carriages	29	Matches	3
Clocks	2	Paper	3
Iron	8	Powder flasks	2
Bolts, nuts,		Eyeglasses	2
screws	5	Water pipes	1
Locks	3	Brass foundries	8
Wire	1	Candles	1
Optical instr.	1	Chairs	2
Plows	1	Firearms	3
Railroad signals	1	Bits	1
Tape measures	1	Railroad frogs	1
Whips	1	Pumps	2
Boilers	3	Pianos	3
Buckles	1	Paper Boxes	2
Carriage parts	11	Steam heating	2
Coffee pots	1	Wheels	3
Axles	1		

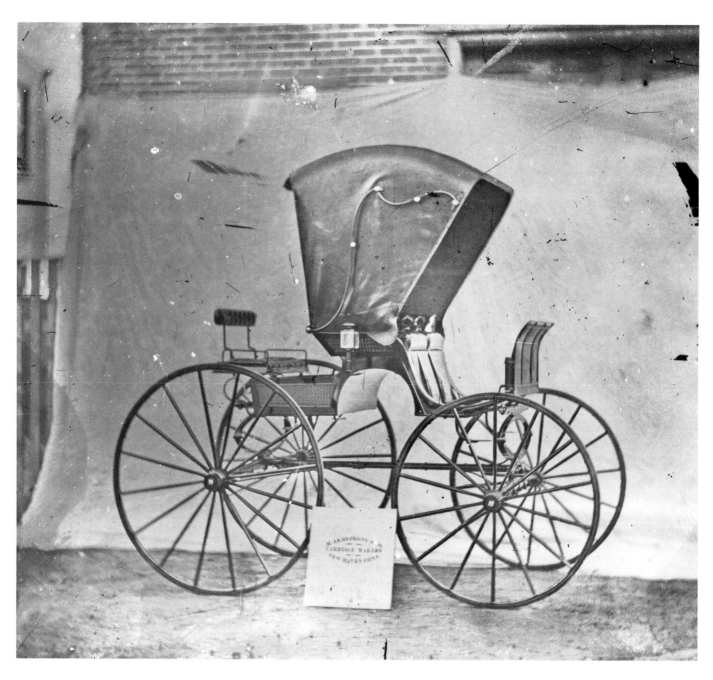

The shift to heavy industry is evident. Fifty years later some 550 companies, employing 28,000 men and women who produced more than 250 different major articles were enumerated.

The carriage industry. The New Haven carriage industry is of special interest to industrial historians because of its early use of machinery to increase efficiency and to cut costs. John Cook, the first of these carriage makers, produced chaises as early as 1794. He was soon followed by other craftsmen who, with simple hand tools, fashioned all the parts of their carriages. Within a few years, specialist firms were formed

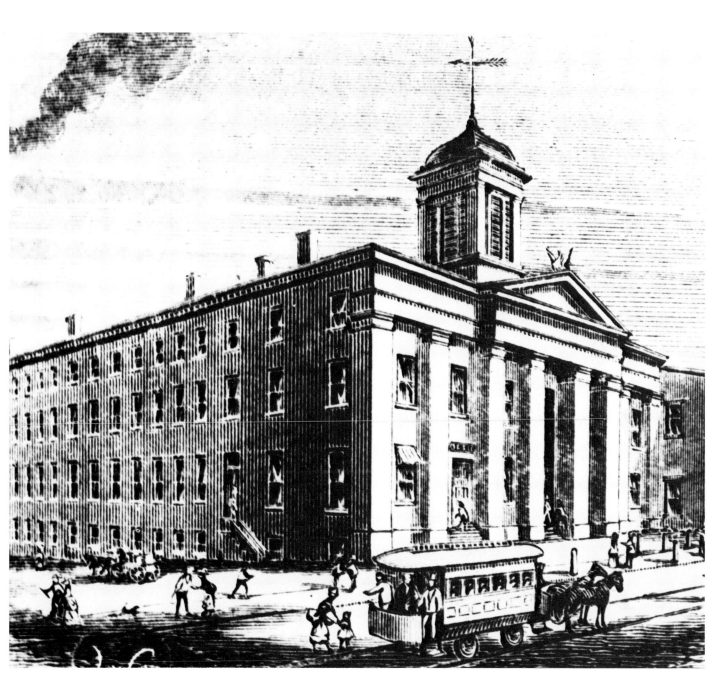

to make axles, wheels, and other components at a lower cost. Although James Brewster, the most famous of the New Haven carriage makers, was the largest, and George T. Newhall showed that steam power on a large scale reduced costs and increased production, true mass production of carriages was first introduced by G & D Cook and Co., who, a few years before the Civil War, successfully increased production from one to 10 carriages a day.

Strong as the carriage industry appeared to be in 1893 when five New Haven firms won prizes at the Columbian Exposition in Chicago, it expired a few years later, unable to compete with the automobile. C. Cowles and Company, one of the winners, founded in 1838, is still in business in New Haven, having successfully shifted to manufacture of specialized automobile parts.

The 19th century was a kind of industrial Paleozoic era in which small shops grew, flourished, and then, struck by economic catastrophes or by the passing of the guiding hand, perished, leaving a few adaptable survivors behind. New Haven's carriage industry, for many years one of the nation's largest, is a prime example of the rise and

Carriages produced at James Brewster's factory on Wooster Street were purchased by Presidents Andrew Jackson and Martin Van Buren.

Facing page
Top
This extremely rare photograph of a carriage from the M. Armstrong company was probably made for advertising purposes in the 1860s.

Bottom
G. and D. Cook's factory on State Street between Wall and Grove was the first to apply mass-production techniques to carriage manufacturing.
(NHCHS)

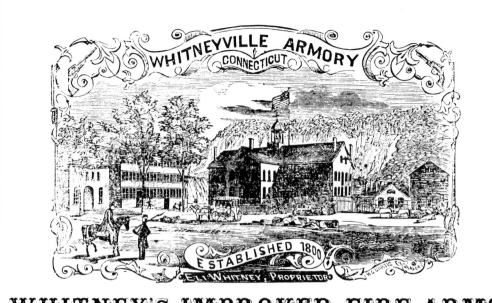

WHITNEY'S IMPROVED FIRE-ARMS.

Top

In 1888 Eli Whitney III rented the Whitney Armory to the Winchester Arms Company for the manufacture of .22 caliber rifles. This engraving shows the Armory's main building, which was erected in 1860, before the transfer. From the Dana Collection. (NHCHS)

Right

This patent model of the cotton gin is one of five that Eli Whitney made or had made before 1800. Whitney's economic losses on the cotton gin were recouped by his gun factory on the Mill River. (NHCHS)

fall of an entire industry.

Eli Whitney and the arms industry. New Haven's status as one of the major arms-manufacturing centers of the United States must be credited to the inventive genius of Eli Whitney, to his long struggle to make his cotton gin a commercial success, and to the innovative gun factory which he designed and built.

Despite severe illness brought on by his bitter experience with the cotton gin, Whitney emerged with a reputation as an inventor and with some understanding of "mass production," knowledge which was useful when he turned to his next project, guns for the federal government. Although lacking gun-making experience, he had influential friends and persistence, and was awarded a two-year contract for 10,000 muskets, a contract which was impossible to fulfill by the traditional method of making guns one at a time, fabricating each part as needed. Whitney planned to build machines to eliminate laborious and time-consuming hand labor, but his ambitious plan took much longer than either he or the government anticipated. The last batch of muskets was not delivered until 1809, 11 years later, because Whitney was forced to design and build machines

which existed only in his imagination and, after they were built, to train workmen to use them.

Eli Whitney has been called the inventor of mass production, but this claim cannot be strictly accurate. Little is known about his machinery, even though his vision is clear. How much influence on mass production did he have? This is still a matter of debate, but it is certain that the precision tools needed to fabricate the completely interchangeable parts required for mass production were not available to him, and it was not until the middle of the 19th century that such machine tools were built.

The Winchester Arms Company, which bought the Whitney Arms Company in 1888, was for many years the largest employer in the city, and later, as a division of the Olin Corporation, continued as a major gun manufacturer.

Other famous New Haven gun factories were established by John M. Marlin in 1870, and by O. F. Mossberg in 1919. These companies, now located in North Haven, will continue the long tradition of New Haven gun making.

Hardware. New Haven was known in industrial circles for more than guns and carriages. As early as 1854 a British Parliamentary Commission praised the

The High Standard Manufacturing Company was one of several local firms engaged in the arms industry. Their Hamden plant was designed by the engineering firm of Westcott and Mapes, founded in 1914. Courtesy, Westcott and Mapes.

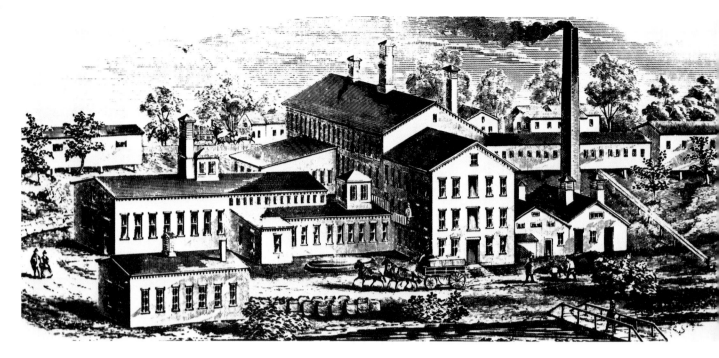

Davenport and Mallory Company's machines which made interchangeable parts for its padlocks. This company produced 2,000 padlocks a day to sell for *five* cents each; a dozen locks, each with a different key, cost the buyer 50 cents. Its successor, Mallory–Wheeler, survived until 1913.

Many other hardware manufacturers flourished in New Haven in the 19th century. The H. B. Ives Company, founded in 1876 to make mortise bolts, is still a major New Haven industry. Leadership in hardware soon passed to J. B. Sargent and Company, which opened for business in New Haven in 1864 on Water Street. After World War II, Sargent moved into a new plant where its 1,000 employees produce a variety of architectural hardware for the building trades.

Paper. Good-quality paper for book publishing, letter writing, and newspapers was costly and often unobtainable in 18th-century Connecticut. New Haven's first paper mill was built in Westville in 1776; several other paper mills later occupied this site.

Joseph Parker's mill at Whalley Avenue and Dayton Street at first relied on the traditional method of converting cotton-mill sweepings and rags, but soon installed one of the first Fourdrinier machines in Connecticut to convert bleached wood pulp into rolls of paper. The Parker firm was one of the first major producers of high-quality book paper in the United States. In 1856, however, Parker developed a line of blotting paper which was so superior to imported blotting board that the company specialized thenceforth in blotting paper until it closed in 1969.

Paper pulp and paper box manufacturing soon became important in New Haven, and by 1872 three pulp and two box factories were busy. The first large box factory was built by Daniel and Henry Gladdings in 1857. Later, two New Haven companies joined with several out-of-state companies to form the National Folding Box Company, which built a massive new plant, said to be the world's largest paper box factory, on James Street in 1906. In 1975 this company, controlled by the Federal Paper Board Company, closed. The New Haven Paper Box Company, now in Hamden, is the sole survivor of the 19th-century paper box industry in New Haven.

Matches. Claims have been made that the match industry in the United States grew from the efforts of New Haven men, especially Thomas Sanford, the reputed inventor of the friction match, but this priority is not supported by the evidence. Sanford,

however, in partnership with Anson Beecher, devised a series of machines which cut matchsticks, dipped them into what seems to have been a dangerous solution of carbon disulfide in which an equally dangerous form of phosphorus was dissolved, and packed them into matchboxes which they manufactured. The partners soon combined five different operations into one machine that converted raw lumber into finished, packed matchboxes. In 1881 the Diamond Match Company, in which Beecher had a financial interest, bought his factory, later moving it to Ohio.

Rubber goods. The story of Charles Goodyear, famed inventor of the rubber vulcanizing process, is one of the great epics of industrial invention. In 1834, when Goodyear was 34, he was fascinated by a rubber life preserver displayed in a New York store and was struck by the commercial possibilities of "India rubber." After years of hardship, he perfected a rubber product that would neither melt in the sun's heat nor freeze in winter. Leverett Candee, a Connecticut native, and probably Goodyear's first patent licensee, formed the L. Candee Rubber Company in 1843 to manufacture rubber overshoes.

In 1892 the Candee company, which

Above
Artesian wells supplied 2,500 gallons of water per minute for the enormous James Street factory of the National Folding Box Company. In 1936 the plant was able to boast that it was the second largest tonnage shipper in Connecticut. From the Dana Collection, NHCHS.

Left
The long years spent by Charles Goodyear in the pursuit of a successful formula for curing India rubber were finally rewarded as the result of an accident. In 1839, while in the midst of an argument, Goodyear dropped a sulphur and rubber mixture on a hot stove; this was the beginning of the vulcanization process he finally perfected and patented in 1844. (NHCHS)

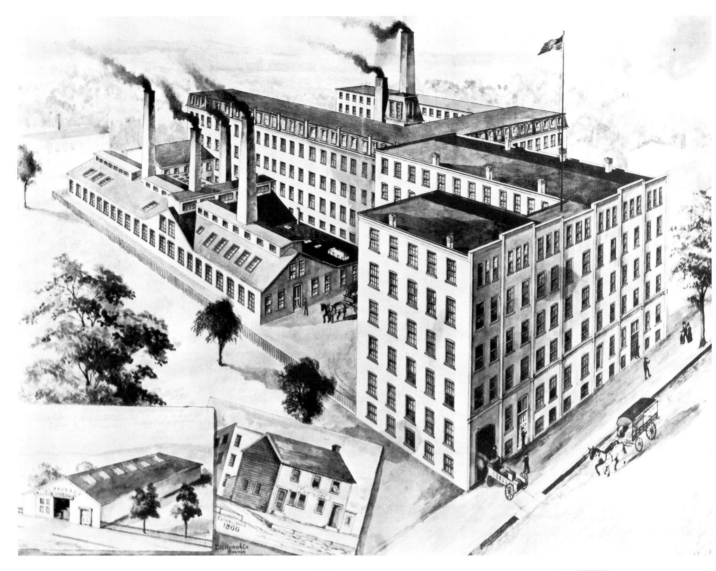

then employed more than 1,000 workers producing thousands of pairs of rubber boots and overshoes each day, was merged into the gigantic United States Rubber Company. At the time, Candee was the third largest rubber factory in the nation. In 1929 the outmoded plant was closed, and the operation moved elsewhere.

Several other small rubber goods manufactories were active in the late 19th century, but only the Seamless

Rubber Company, founded in 1877, became important. Changes in its markets and competition from other manufacturers closed Seamless Rubber after World War II.

Electric power. Waterpower, whose availability attracted manufacturers to Hamden and Westville, was inadequate as factories grew in size; manufacturers now turned to steam power. Although the first steam engine in Connecticut manufacturing was introduced as early as 1811, steam was adopted slowly because waterpower was sufficient for small factories, and suitable fuel for steam engines was often unavailable. By 1838, however, 11 New Haven plants were using steam power, and by 1860 most of the larger factories were fully committed to it.

As steam power, in turn, began to fall short, industry reluctantly turned to the new electric motor. A few New Haveners rose to the challenge of the coming electrical era by incorporating the New Haven Electric Light Company to supply electricity, which they knew would soon be in demand. In 1899 the United Illuminating Company was formed by merger with the Bridgeport Electric Light Company. Local industries were equipping machines with electric motors to give their operators better control and to improve working conditions. However, it was probably the success of the electric streetcars in New Haven which finally convinced industrialists that electric power would serve their needs better than steam power, despite their heavy investment in steam.

The Water Company. Each of New Haven's utilities grew from humble beginnings in the 19th century. Each has a fascinating history. The New Haven Water Company is unique, however, because of the long contest for control of the company by a faction of New Haveners who sought public ownership as against private ownership. This contest has finally been decided in favor of public control by the municipalities served by the water company.

Gas lighting. The oldest utility in

Top
By 1941 the United Illuminating Company had outgrown its Venetian palazzo-style headquarters on the corner of Temple and Crown streets circa 1910. Photo by T. S. Bronson. (NHCHS)

Bottom
George R. Bradley photographed the Mill River dam and buildings of the New Haven Water Company circa 1890. Water from Lake Whitney was pumped to a reservoir on Prospect Hill. (NHCHS)

The Jerome Clock Company established New Haven as a major producer of clocks during the 19th century. The above view of the factory dates from 1850. Below is a spring-driven mantel clock with rosewood veneer manufactured by his firm circa 1860. (NHCHS)

New Haven, now one of the oldest businesses in Connecticut, is a corporation which, for most of its life, was known as the New Haven Gas Company, and is now the Southern Connecticut Gas Company. The first stores and homes in New Haven were connected to gas in November 1848. Durrie and Peck's bookstore was the first commercial establishment to use gas. Benjamin Silliman, Jr., one of the company's founders, saw to it that his home on Hillhouse Avenue was the first house illuminated by gas. Installation of gas street lights, beginning in 1849, soon brightened the city at night. The gas company prospered, serving more than 1,200 customers by 1856, but oil lighting was not replaced by gaslight in most New Haven homes until well after the Civil War.

The telephone. The fourth major utility company in New Haven, the Southern New England Telephone Company, entered into a feeble infancy on January 15, 1878. Alexander Graham Bell's telephone demonstration in New Haven on April 27, 1877, inspired George W. Coy, manager of a local telegraph office, to organize his own telephone business. Eight telephone lines were strung on poles to serve the handful of subscribers when service began on January 28, 1878. Since New Haven was the first city to provide telephone service, commercially produced equip-

ment was unknown; Coy and his assistants made all of it themselves as inexpensively as possible. This equipment was crude and inefficient. The operator who worked the wooden switchboard, for example, had to make six separate connections and disconnections to complete a single call.

By late February 1878, the first telephone directory, listing 50 subscribers, was published; the number of subscribers grew slowly at first, reaching 200 in April 1878, and only 12,000 by 1900.

Clocks. Many of the leaders in the early American clock industry were Connecticut men—Eli Terry, Seth Thomas, Elias Ingraham, William L. Gilbert, and Chauncey Jerome, for example. Jerome, who later served New Haven as mayor, is credited with "the greatest and most far-reaching contribution to the clock industry in Connecticut—that of the substitution of brass works for wooden works."[4] Jerome perfected his brass-works clock before he moved to New Haven, and by 1837 his company was selling a one-day wood-cased clock for $6, and in a year for only $4. In 1845 his Bristol factory burned, and Jerome relocated to a branch plant in New Haven where he sold one line of clocks at a wholesale price of 75 cents. Because of an unfortunate stock involvement with P. T. Barnum, the Jerome Clock Company was forced into bankruptcy. Jerome

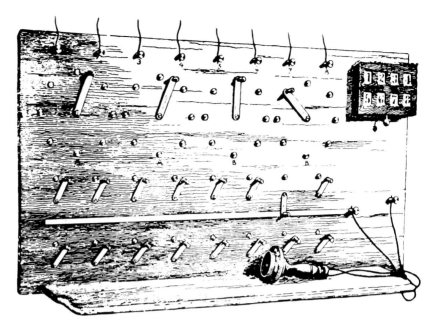

never recovered from this episode. As he ruefully admitted, he was a much better inventor than businessman.

James E. English and Hiram Camp, the latter having founded the New Haven Clock Company which made clock cases, took control of Jerome's company; they built it into the largest clock manufactory in Connecticut and one of the largest in the world. In the 1920s nearly 2,000 men and women turned out more than two million clocks and watches a year. Changing times, stiffer competition, and an antiquated plant eventually weakened the company, which was forced out of business after World War II.

Banking. Since initiative, native intelligence, and business acumen must be combined with capital in an industrial society, New Haven's banking industry played an important part in the rapid growth of industry in the 19th and early 20th centuries. When indus-

Top left
The New Haven Bank was the first in the city. Its building on the corner of Chapel and Orange streets was photographed when vacated for remodeling in 1866.

Top right
Drawing of the world's first telephone switchboard, fabricated by George W. Coy of New Haven. From the Dana Collection, NHCHS.

Above
This circa 1910 night view of the New Haven Gas Company's headquarters on Crown Street dramatically advertised the benefits of gas illumination. (NHCHS)

try was insignificant and commerce depended on a few wealthy men whose money came from land and shipping, banks were not needed. It was not until 1795 that the first bank in New Haven, appropriately named the New Haven Bank, was organized. The second one, the Eagle Bank, which opened in 1811, failed in 1825 because of poor management. The New Haven Savings Bank, one of the few still conducting business under its original name, was founded in 1838.

By 1946, more than 30 banks were in business in New Haven and its contiguous towns, 10 of which are still in existence. In 1981 the New Haven region is served by more than a hundred banks and bank branches.

Other New Haven industry. The roster of historically important companies in New Haven's industrial growth is too long to be given the detailed attention it deserves. But surely the Greist Manufacturing Company should be mentioned. Founded in Westville in 1870 to make sewing-machine attachments, Greist has successfully shifted to new lines of manufactured goods. Its neighbor across Fitch Street, the Geometric Tool Company, moved in 1893 to New Haven where Howard E. Adt developed specialized machine tools which established the company as a leader in the machine-tool industry.

The Whitney Avenue–Audubon Street section was, for many years, the center of the foundry and machine-shop trade in the city. More than 20 large and small companies such as H. B. Bigelow, D. Frisbie, Whitney Root, Calhoun and Root, W. J. Smith,

New Haven Manufacturing, W. G. Maltby, Cyprian Wilcox, S. H. Barnum, Climax Pin, and the McLagon Foundry were located there at one time or another. The Eastern Elevator Company, now at Hamilton Street, was also established in this district as the Audubon Machine Company, manufacturing elevators, brickmaking equipment, and hoisting machinery.

In 1861, Hobart Bigelow, a skilled machinist, later mayor of New Haven, founded the Bigelow Company in the machine-shop section. By 1870, growing business forced a move to River and Lloyd streets where the company is still in business. Although Bigelow originally manufactured portable steam engines, sugarmill machinery, and boilers for the West Indian sugar industry as its main line, it has successfully specialized for many years in fabricating and erecting large steam boilers for major industries.

The A. W. Flint Company on Chapel Street, which was always a small business, deserves to be singled out because it is 100 years old, having been founded by Adelbert W. Flint in 1880 to make ladders and lawn and porch furniture, and still makes ladders and staging, which are marketed throughout the East.

Economists and industrial historians may not agree, but many New Haveners still mourn the disappearance of the A. C. Gilbert Company. Alfred Carleton Gilbert, its founder, started out to manufacture sets of magic tricks in 1909 under the name of Mysto Magic. Successful in this, Gilbert, seeking new toys to add to his line, invented the Erector Set which he first exhibited to the public in 1913. It immediately captivated children and parents. In 1916, when his annual sales exceeded a million dollars, Gilbert changed his corporate name to the A. C. Gilbert Company, and moved to a larger building at Blatchley Avenue and Peck Street, adding new toys and electrical appliances to his product line.

Mr. Gilbert's death in 1961, followed soon after by that of his son, in combination with a changing toy market, forced A. C. Gilbert and Company to close in 1967, although, happily, "Erector" sets are still manufactured.

Industry in neighboring towns. Industrial development in Hamden was surprisingly diversified. During the 19th century, Hamden's factories produced carriage hardware, industrial webbing, sleigh bells, boxes, silk, carpets, rubber products, bullets, fertilizer from menhaden, a marine fish, and from slaughterhouse wastes (this plant, fortunately, was situated in a remote district of Mount Carmel), a variety of industrial and household hardware, small tools, matches, and needles.

The Moran Company, one of the longest-lived companies in the region, was founded in Troy, New York, in 1869 and was established in New Haven in 1880. Moran moved to Hamden in 1950 when its New Haven plant burned down. Still managed and controlled by the Moran family, now in the fifth generation, the Moran Company has specialized in brushes and brooms for industrial and food services for more than a century.

Industry in other neighboring towns was less diversified. The West Haven Buckle Company, 1853, and the American Buckle Company, established in upstate Connecticut in 1843 and relocated to West Haven in 1885, are still active, although their product lines have changed over the years.

The Malleable Iron Fittings Company, founded in 1855 in Branford, was one of the earliest malleable iron foundries in the United States. Its chemical control and research laboratory, organized in 1875, was the first laboratory of its kind in the malleable iron industry. The company ceased operation in 1969.

The Henry G. Thompson Company in Branford, also more than 100 years old, was founded in 1876, moved to New Haven in 1880, and then back to Branford where its 200 employees continue to make industrial saw blades.

Labor. The life of the 19th-century laborer was hard. Hours were long;

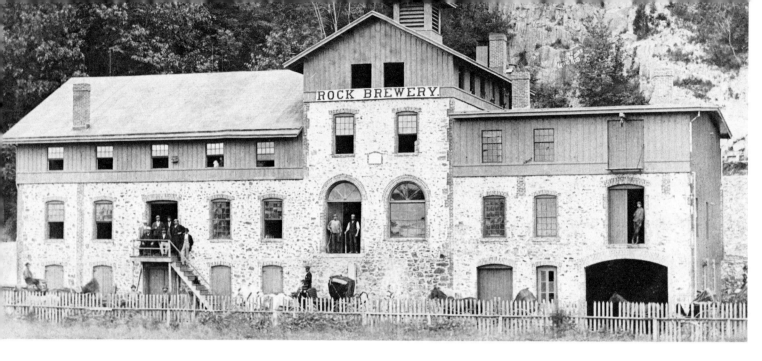

pay, often in goods, was low; pensions and retirement systems unheard of. The worker's education was rudimentary, usually ending with grammar school. Illness struck both rich and poor but struck the poor far more often and far more catastrophically. The skilled mechanic was at least one economic step above the laborer. Many mechanics rose to own their own companies, but skilled or not, working men, women, and children found life difficult.

Some New Haven leaders, concerned about the living and working conditions of their employees, organized the New Haven Mutual Aid Association in 1833 to help distressed young workers and their families. Even earlier, the General Society of Mechanics of New Haven was established in 1807 "to promote and regulate the mechanic arts" and to make loans to apprentices and donations to "worthy paupers." The Mutual Benevolent Society of Cordwainers of New Haven, organized in 1821, was the first strong labor group, perhaps because it excluded masters from membership.

Education was one key to moving up in society, but it was difficult for young mechanics to attend school while working 60 hours or more a week. Self-improvement was almost as difficult, since the New Haven Public Library did not open until 1887, although two private library companies, both dating from the beginning of the 19th century, were available upon payment of membership fees which few workers could afford.

James Brewster, the carriage maker, recognized their plight and organized the Young Mechanics' Institute where workers could hear lectures on topics of interest to them. In 1831 he established a Lyceum, open to all, in a building he purchased at Church and Crown streets, bearing all costs himself. By the standards of his time, Brewster was an enlightened employer. He paid his workers in cash instead of the detested orders for goods. Keenly aware of the pernicious effects of liquor on workers, he barred alcoholic drink from his factory, contrary to New Haven custom, and despite his reputation as a strict and demanding employer, he was said to attract the best mechanics to his shop.

As industry grew larger and national in scope, labor formed stronger associations. Through the efforts of such groups as the 500-man coachmaker's union, the eight-hour workday law was eventually passed. By the turn of the 20th century, the skilled trades were well organized. The majority of factory workers in New Haven, however, were not unionized

Inventor Eli Whitney Blake, shown here with an unidentified niece, is best remembered for his stone crusher, patented in 1858. Crushed stone for macadam roads was originally produced by workmen with sledgehammers. The lower construction cost made possible by Blake's labor-saving machine stimulated the transportation of men and materials. From the Dana Collection, NHCHS.

until after World War II when, for the first time, large numbers of working women were enrolled.

Epilogue. Industry in Connecticut and in the New Haven region developed slowly, but when the Industrial Revolution hit, its impact was overwhelming, profoundly altering a way of life that would have been familiar in the 17th century. When it came, Connecticut and New Haven were in the forefront. New Haven seems to have been destined for industrial leadership because its capitalists, men like Leverett Candee and Ebenezer Beecher, took advantage of the ingenuity and ability of such New Haven inventors as Charles Goodyear, Eli Whitney, Eli Whitney Blake, Ebenezer Chittenden, Alexander C. Twining, Joseph Parker, Philos Blake, Henry Parmalee, Jonathan Mix, and, much later, J. Allen Heaney, to name but a few.

Since change is the only constant in life, the industrial focus of the 19th century, carriage making, rubber shoes, paper boxes, guns, and hardware, soon shifted to a different product mix, and within recent years, to manufacture in one-story buildings in city-sponsored industrial parks. New industries, such as the highly automated electronics and printing firms, are much less labor intensive, relying on a relatively small number of highly skilled employees.

Employment has shifted from manufacturing to such service occupations as the enormous health industry created by a new social ethos, to new state and federal jobs, to stores large and small in shopping centers large and small, and to work in the many financial, insurance, and real-estate companies of the region.

Contrary to popular belief, heavy industry has always been mobile. For more than a century, companies moved from New Haven and from Connecticut for a variety of reasons, perhaps to be closer to raw materials or to lower labor costs or lower energy costs, or because of antiquated plants or lack of land or financial reorganization—usually leaving their workers behind to shift for themselves.

But industry has also moved to Connecticut and to New Haven, and continues to move here, attracted by a pool of skilled workers, good school systems, the cultural and technical resources of Yale University and the other local colleges, and the availability of excellent transportation. These new industries, however, are very different from the pioneers which built the old factories, and they will surely change in ways that cannot be anticipated as the 20th century draws to a close.

Chapter VI

THE SOCIAL HISTORY OF NEW HAVEN

by Judith A. Schiff

In the 19th and early 20th centuries New Haven was the scene of much activity on the part of womens-rights groups. In September of 1916, 4,000 women from all parts of the state of Connecticut marched in New Haven to publicize the right to vote by women. After the parade these suffragettes carried their message to the workers at the Winchester Arms Company. Photo by Joseph Candee. (NHCHS)

They are Govern'd by the same Laws as wee in Boston, . . . And much the same way of Church Government, and many of them good, Sociable people, and I hope Religious too: but a little too much Independent in their principalls.

(Journal of Madam Knight, 1704)

Some of the earliest written observations of New Haven society were made by Sarah Kemble Knight, who traveled from Boston to New Haven in the fall of 1704. Madam Knight (a title bestowed for her distinction as a schoolteacher), who made the arduous journey on horseback to attend to an estate matter, was taken care of in New Haven by her kinsman, Mr. Thomas Trowbridge. The settling of the estate took some time which afforded Sarah Knight ample time to inform herself "of the manners and customs of the place."[1] But, she was most favorably impressed with the abundance and quality of the oysters, one of the features which enabled the people of New Haven to live "very well and comfortably in their famelies."[2] And also, according to the outspoken journalist's standards, they were "too indulgent (especially the farmers) to their slaves: sufering too great familiarity from them, permitting them to sit at Table and eat with them, (as they say to save time,) and into the dish goes the black hoof as freely as the white hand."[3]

The social relations of the New Haven citizenry with the native and black populations were remarkable for the time. In matters of legal differences and criminal acts the non-white residents were given equal consideration by the judges. An example of this objectivity was also recounted by Madam Knight, which involved a farmer, "who had some difference with his slave, concerning something the master had promised him and did not punctualy perform; which caused some harsh words between them; But at length they put the matter to Arbitration and Bound themselves to stand to the award of such as they named—which done, the Arbitrators Having heard the Allegations of both parties, Order the master to pay 40 shillings to black face, and acknowledge his fault, And so the matter ended; the poor master very honestly standing to the award."[4]

Humane and equal treatment before the law, however, did not imply that democracy prevailed in the Puritan colony. When the planters founded their new haven in the wilderness, it was to ensure their right to live by God's law as they would rightly interpret it. From 1638 until well into the 19th century, social equality and political power were enjoyed only by members of the congregation.

When the Puritans settled in New Haven, they were fortunate to find a

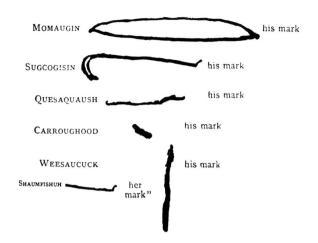

MOMAUGIN	his mark
SUGCOGISIN	his mark
QUESAQUAUSH	his mark
CARROUGHOOD	his mark
WEESAUCUCK	his mark
SHAUMPISHUH	her mark"

The holdings of Shaumpishuh, sister of Momauguin, extended from East Haven to Guilford. As a member of Momauguin's council, her mark was required on the deed that conveyed the lands of the Quinnipiacs to the founders of the New Haven Colony. From Atwater, History of the Colony of New Haven, *1902.*

Facing page
Above
Benjamin Silliman, Sr., the "Father of American Scientific Education," was offered the first professorship in science at Yale despite his lack of scientific training. (NHCHS)

Below
A brick building on the corner of High and Wall streets housed the Hopkins Grammar School beginning in 1873. Hopkins sold the property to Yale which demolished the building in 1929 for the Sterling Law Quadrangle. (NHCHS)

dwindling native population, debilitated and war weary. The Quinnipiac sachems readily agreed to live harmoniously with the English and moved their people into what is considered to be the first Indian reservation in the United States. The Indians gave up their lands primarily in exchange for protection against the Pequots, Mohawks, and other Indians. It is most remarkable that one of the negotiating sachems was a woman, Shaumpishuh, sister of Momauguin, chief of the Quinnipiacs, and herself the sachem-squaw of Guilford. Her impressive holdings, known as Menunkatuck, which extended from Kuttanoo in East Haven to the East River in Guilford, brought the same price in goods as did the sale of New Haven.

The Indians lived on their reservation of 30 acres for a period of about 130 years. In 1768 the few remaining Quinnipiacs moved to Farmington among the Tunxis tribe, purchasing their land with the proceeds of the sale of the East Shore reservation. In summing up the story of the colonists' relations with the Indians, John William De Forest, the distinguished New Haven writer, mused on the fate of the Connecticut Indians:

Knowing little of European modes of life, and judging of the colonists greatly by themselves, they supposed that the latter would cultivate but a little land, and support themselves, for the rest, by trading, fishing and hunting. Little did they think, that in the course of years the white population would increase from scores to hundreds, and from hundreds to thousands; that the deep forests would be cut down; that the wild animals would disappear; that the fish would grow few in the rivers; and that the poor remnant of the Quinnipiacs would eventually leave the graves of their forefathers, and wander away into another land. Could they have anticipated that a change so wonderful, and, in their history, so unprecedented, would of necessity follow the coming of the white man, they would have preferred the wampum tributes of the Pequots and the scalping parties of the Five Nations, to the vicinity of a people so kind, so peaceable and yet so destructive.

Notwithstanding, De Forest realistically concluded that "the puritans of the New Haven colony are perhaps not less worthy of praise than the quakers of Philadelphia for the peace and quietness which invariably existed between them and the aborigines."[5]

As the prime reason for the establishment of the New Haven colony was religion, the primary characteristic that shaped its history was education. To the Puritans, education was needed on two levels: first, to provide a level of literacy to enable every inhabitant to read the Bible; and second, to train young men to lead the colony as clergy and professional men. The strong de-

sire to train and be led by men of their own kind led to the founding of Yale. It persisted up through the 19th century, and a striking example was noted by Benjamin Silliman in his "Reminiscences." At the beginning of the 19th century, Yale President Timothy Dwight asked Silliman to accept the first professorship in science, although Silliman was not trained in science. Dwight stated that it was "impossible to find, among us, a man properly qualified, but that he would prefer to select "one of our own young men, born & trained among us & possessed of our habits and sympathies," and "enable him to acquire the requisite science and skill." He remarked moreover, according to Silliman, "that a foreigner, with his peculiar habits and prejudices, would not feel and act in unison with us."

In removing from Boston to Quinnipiac in 1638, the Puritans brought a schoolteacher, Ezekiel Cheever, who established a school in his own home. Within a few years a schoolhouse was built on the Green and supported with public and private funds. The death of Edward Hopkins, a wealthy London merchant and an uncle of Elihu Yale, brought a bequest of £400 which endowed the Hopkins Grammar School. Since 1660 this school has continued to flourish, and in recent years merged with the girls' school, Day-Prospect Hill. Hopkins, originally a member of the Davenport-Eaton group, had in-

stead settled at Hartford where he served as governor and deputy-governor for nearly 15 years. When his wife, Anne Yale Hopkins, became deranged, according to Governor Winthrop's journal, from too much reading and writing, Hopkins returned with her to England. The year after his death in 1656, Hopkins' mother-in-law, Mrs. Anne Yale Eaton, Governor Eaton's widow, who had been excommunicated by the Reverend Davenport and the church elders, also returned to England. Her son, David Yale, and small grandson, Elihu Yale, accompanied her. Sixty years later, the grandson, who had become a wealthy entrepreneur in the India trade, gave a large benefaction to the Collegiate School in New Haven which has since borne his name. The prophecy of the shrewd fund-raiser, Cotton Mather, who promised Elihu Yale that his gift would memorialize his name better than an Egyptian pyramid, has indeed been fulfilled.

Unfortunately the fine education provided by the Grammar and Collegiate Schools was not available to all. In colonial times, girls and many boys received their entire education in "dame schools." They were small private schools operated by women in their own homes for groups of eight to 10 small children. The curriculum con-

sisted primarily of manners of behavior and basic reading taught with the aid of a hornbook. In 1795 the state school fund was provided with money from the sale of land in the Western Reserve. Administered by James Hillhouse, the fund enabled local schools to flourish, but after the War of 1812 they entered a period of decline. While the children of the middle and upper classes attended expensive private academies, needy children were receiving little schooling and of poor quality. To remedy the situation an innovative Lancastrian School was opened in 1822 in which expenses were minimized by using older students as teaching assistants. Despite its success, an investigative report of 1831 revealed that only one-third of the 2,682 school-age children (4 to 16) were attending school. Of this number, one-half were enrolled in inferior schools. A movement to establish graded schools in New Haven resulted in the opening of the first grade school in 1853, named after Noah Webster, a distinguished resident and founder of the Society for the Improvement of Common Schools.

Education for black residents dated from 1811 with the opening of the first "colored school." Among the charity schools, which were privately operated by women reformers prior to the development of the public school system,

was one integrated school. Even the public education system provided only two primary-level schools for Negroes. One student at Sally Wilson's Artisan Street Colored School, Edward Bouchet, became the first black person to earn the Ph.D. degree in the United States. Bouchet's father came to New Haven in 1824 as the "body servant" of John B. Robertson, a Yale freshman from Charleston, South Carolina. Robertson and Bouchet remained in New Haven, both married, and had sons of the same age. Edward Bouchet, born in 1852, graduated from Hopkins Grammar School as valedictorian. Entering Yale barely five years after the Civil War, he was graduated with highest honors, a member of Phi Beta Kappa, and the first black graduate of the college. Bouchet went on to study science in the graduate school; he received his doctorate in the centennial year, 1876. Bouchet spent much of his professional life as a teacher in Philadelphia, but was also known as a "walking encyclopedia of New Haven people and events." Dedicated to the betterment of his own people, Bouchet was an active member of the NAACP. In 1918, he died at his home on Bradley Street and was buried in Evergreen Cemetery.

While Bouchet was a student at Yale, the college became the beneficiary of a bequest of Mary Goodman,

a black resident of New Haven. She left her entire estate to establish a scholarship fund for black students in the Yale Divinity School. In 1872 the sum of $5,000 was realized from the sale of her property and this fund exists today. In recognition of her great gift, the Yale Corporation voted to bury Mrs. Goodman in the "college lot" in Grove Street Cemetery. Her gravestone still reads clearly: "Mary A. Goodman, of African descent, who gave the earnings of her life to educate men of her own color in Yale College for the Gospel ministry."

The decade following the Civil War was marked by social change. In Connecticut, where slavery had been gradually eliminated at the end of the 18th century, the most profound change was seen in the activities and status of women. Married women had taken over the running of their husbands' businesses when they were called away to serve. Single women worked in the South as teachers to the newly emancipated black population. Many women served as nurses and fund-raisers. In 1869 the Connecticut Woman Suffrage Association was founded with the sponsorship of Susan B. Anthony and Isabella Beecher Hooker. Bills were introduced in 1870 at the state legislature to extend the franchise to women, and it was at the State House on the New Haven Green that the woman suffrage bill was launched. Hopes ran high, especially because New Haven's first woman minister, Phoebe Hanaford, had been appointed Chaplain to open the session of the state assembly. Phoebe Hanaford's Sunday services at the Universalist Church were so popular that crowds stood at the rear of the overflowing hall. But the innovation of a woman opening an assembly meeting proved to be only a courtesy when the

bill was defeated. New Haven women would have to wait 20 years, until 1892, when the state allowed women to vote in school-board elections. The *New York Times* reported on the election in New Haven, which provided the first opportunity for Connecticut women to vote. When the polls opened at 6 a.m., women had been lined up for hours in order to ensure that a woman cast the first ballot.

During this period women also were admitted to some previously all-male colleges. Even Yale briefly considered the possibility of becoming coed, but did not accept the policy for the undergraduate college for another century. In 1870, the only coeducational school at Yale was the Art School, followed by the Music School and the Graduate School in 1892. The majority of students in the Art School were New Haven women. Local women also had some access to a Yale education through popular lecture series which professors taught to supplement their incomes. As early as 1808 Professor Benjamin Silliman taught a full course in chemistry that was open to women, whom he considered the intellectual equals of men.

The presence of Yale in New Haven brought many social benefits. Often graduates would choose to remain there to practice their professions or start businesses. Visiting scholars and dignitaries were added attractions. Daughters of professors, the clergy, and other residents often found suitable matches among the student body. New Haveners were also exposed to faraway cultures through representatives who were brought to Yale as students by alumni missionaries. In 1809 a Hawaiian youth, Henry Obookiah, came to New Haven and lived in President Timothy Dwight's home for a

considerable period. West Indians and South Americans appeared as students even in the 18th century. In the fall of 1850 the first Chinese student, Yung Wing, enrolled at Yale, and after his graduation, worked to enable many other Chinese youths to be educated at Yale and other New England schools. Soon after, Japanese students appeared in New Haven, and as the Yale-trained missionaries stationed themselves around the globe, new students arrived from the Near and Middle East.

Social exposure to the student body proved to be a mixed blessing, however, as New Haveners had unhappy experiences with the Yale students. Sailors and the less privileged young men of the town began to be involved in gang fighting with the students after the Revolution. A confrontation with clubs and knives occurred in 1812 which was said to have involved 400 on each side (something of an exaggeration as the entire student body was about 300). Soon after the establishment of the Medical School in 1813, townsfolk began to suspect the medical students of body-snatching and grave-robbing. In 1824, the shocking news that the body of a young woman had been taken from the West Haven cemetery to the Medical School spread throughout the two communities. Enraged residents besieged the Medical School for five nights in a row. The constable, Erastus Osborn, in a letter to his father, Shadrack, the postmaster of Southbury, wrote that "people were wrought up to a great pitch, and the Town is full of stories. Hardly a person here has lost friends for Months back but what has been to enquire of me if I did not see them at the College."

Two tragic, "town-gown" confrontations occurred in the 1850s during the

The first department to admit women at Yale was the Art School. George R. Bradley photographed ivy-covered Street Hall, the home of the Art School, about 1890. (NHCHS)

Mrs. Walter Camp watched over Yale football practices when her husband was unable to attend. Her knowledge of the game equaled that of her husband, who credited her as the source for several new rules. From the Walter Camp Papers, Yale University Library.

presidency of Theodore Dwight Woolsey. In 1854, after a performance in Homan's Athenaeum, a mob followed a group of 50 or 60 students back to the campus. A protective constable kept the taunting "townies" away until the "gownies" bravely burst into the traditional student song, "Gaudeamus Igitur," as they reached the Upper Green. The mob threw bricks from a nearby construction site and the students who carried pistols returned with a volley of gun shot. In the confusion the mob leader, Patrick O'Neill, was stabbed to death. The students then barricaded themselves in a dormitory where they were saved from cannon attack by the police. The guilty party was never found out. In 1858 the students had a violent confrontation with the local fire company which resulted in the fatal shooting of a fireman. Again the student responsible was not discovered, but from that time Yale students were forbidden to carry any weapon.

For 60 years thereafter, there were no major incidents. Then a most unfortunate town-gown battle took place in May 1919 when the 102nd Infantry returned to New Haven. As the veterans paraded past the campus, insults were exchanged about the relative contribution of each group to the war effort. The next day, further verbal exchanges led to a march on Yale by 300 veterans and 5,000 residents. Students, safely locked behind the iron gates of the Old Campus, were exposed only to volleys of rocks which smashed dormitory windows. If anyone resembling a student was found in town, he was severely beaten during the rioting. On the third day, the town mob was met by armed state guardsmen and doused by firehoses. The last confrontation of a serious nature was the St. Patrick's Day riot of 1959 which involved students and policemen who were marching in the parade. Students gave in to the irresistible combination of curbside snowbanks and the convenient targets marching by. The re-

sulting melee ended in many injuries and 41 arrests.

The mainstream of New Haven history however, usually flowed without turbulence. Yale enriched New Haven and provided an accessible avenue of upward mobility for its burgeoning immigrant population. As Yale grew larger it was relatively inexpensive to enroll as a day student, and among the many New Haveners who roomed at home was Valentine Giamatti, father of Yale President A. Bartlett Giamatti. In the late 19th century, more and more sons of the affluent Gilded Age appeared as well. Furnishing the handsome gentlemen's quarters in the dormitories or private apartments with pianos, fur rugs, and Tiffany lamps, they used the services of local laundrywomen, sweeps, and cooks. Students sat on the Yale Fence at the corner of Chapel and College streets seeing all and being seen. As team sports grew in importance, the football, baseball, and crew heroes became celebrities of local and

national importance. Walter Camp, a former football star, coached and developed football at Yale, while directing the work of the New Haven Clock Company. When business kept him away from the football field, Mrs. Camp observed and reported on the plays, and was credited by her husband with the formulation of some rules. Football was supported by the town as well as by the college. In the days of carriages, attending a football game in a large coach became fashionable. In the 20th century fans were crammed into open-sided trolley cars which clanged and clattered their way from the Green to the monumental Yale Bowl. The pre-game festivities at the Bowl in the post-World War II era, came to be as important as the game itself, as parties crowded around wooden-sided station wagons for food and drink. As with football, tail-gating may not have been invented in New Haven, but the art developed here to stand as a model for the world .

The complicated rules that governed who could and who could not sit on "The Fence" were quickly forgotten by Yale students when an attractive woman appeared. T. S. Bronson recorded the phenomenon during commencement exercises in June of 1908. (NHCHS)

"Edgewood," Donald Grant Mitchell's home in Westville, was immortalized in Mitchell's series of popular books published during the 19th century. The house where Mitchell worked out his designs for many of New Haven's parks still stands although its appearance has been altered considerably since this photograph was taken before Mitchell's death in 1908. Photo by Myron W. Filley. (NHCHS)

Facing page
Top
The events available to New Haven's citizens on their days off included bicycle races. Dentist William Starr Horton snapped these competitors at Yale Field, circa 1905. (NHCHS)

Middle
Refreshments served at the Pavilion were an incentive for an excursion to the summit of East Rock. (NHCHS)

Bottom
Momaugin's beaches continue to attract a loyal following year after year. Dancing in Swift's Colonnade was among the pleasures available to these sun worshipers in July of 1909. Photo by T. S. Bronson. (NHCHS)

Recreation has assumed a great importance in New Haven life. Probably the geography that brings most New Haveners in daily visual contact with the water and East and West Rocks is a contributing factor. From early days, both rich and poor New Haveners have had ready access to salt- and fresh-water bathing, hiking, skating, fishing, and boating. The nearby beaches of Lighthouse, Fort Hale, Savin Rock, Woodmont, Double Beach, Short Beach, Mansfield Grove, and many others provided seasonal pleasures that are forever preserved in old photographs and postcards. Of these, Savin Rock in West Haven provided the greatest attractions in the form of resort hotels, seafood restaurants, an amusement park, and the dancing pavilions that played a part in the nurturing of such outstanding musicians of the Big Band era as Rudy Vallee, Charlie Spivak, and Artie Shaw.

The very heart of New Haven is itself a public parkland and continues to be the most important community recreation area in the city. Early beautification of New Haven centered on the improvement of the Green. In the last quarter of the 18th century, the Green was transformed through the efforts of James Hillhouse from a congested eyesore to a lovely park. To en-sure its continuous improvement, an ordinance was passed in 1798 to protect the Green from the principal causes of anxiety: unruly geese and Yale students. As the stately elms grew to dominate the Green, the popular author Louisa Tuthill dubbed New Haven the City of Elms. The Upper Green housed the three historic churches and the State House that stood there from 1828 to 1889. Shaded benches beckoned the passerby to enjoy the concerts performed on the bandstand on the Lower Green. A more active recreation also thrived there. The well-known Doolittle view of Yale's Old Brick Row in 1807 is memorable as Yale students played football on the Upper Green. Paved walkways served as paths for the first bicycle craze in 1869, known as velocipedemania. And in the 19th century the Lower Green was flooded to form a skating rink. In 1887, Harriet Terry, former Lady Principal of Vassar and sister of the famous General Alfred Howe Terry of New Haven, praised the beauty of New Haven in a letter to her sisters:

I wish you girls could be here with us. New Haven never was so beautiful before. I do not mean that it is merely more beautiful to my eyes, but it is actually more beautiful than ever. The trees have grown

& are kept in perfect condition, no worms, even in June, and the streets are clean as they can be, while the passion for ornamenting private grounds has seized all the people owning grounds of any size. It is without question the prettiest town I was ever in.

During war years patriotism was inspired by regular military drills, marches, and parades on the Green. In the early years of World War II, spirits were lifted by the sound of the Army Air Force band conducted by Glenn Miller, who was stationed at Yale University.

After the success of the design and creation of Central Park in New York City was recognized, the park movement developed in many cities. In New Haven the leading park planner was Donald Grant Mitchell, better known by his pen name, Ik Marvel. In 1855 he purchased a farm in the Westville secton of New Haven and named it Edgewood. The 360-acre farm became a model described in a series of books, including *My Farm at Edgewood* and *Wet Days at Edgewood*, which attracted visitors from all over America. In addition to the beautification of the Westville area, Mitchell was the planner of the East Rock, Fort Hale, and Bayview parks. After Mitchell's death in 1908,

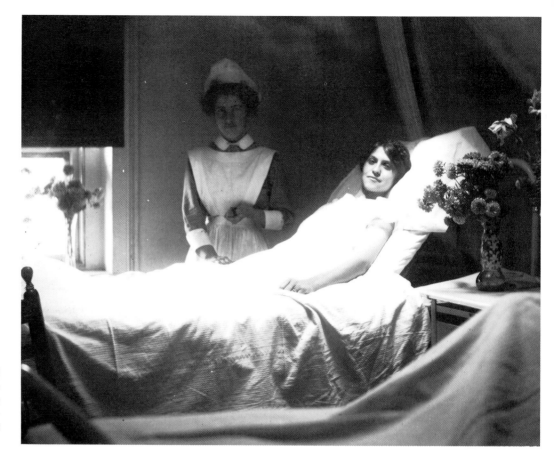

Right
On-the-job training was provided by the Connecticut Training School for Nurses at New Haven Hospital. An unidentified student monitors a patient's pulse circa 1915. (NHCHS)

Below
George Dudley Seymour considered this 1895 portrait "the best picture I ever had taken—by George C. Cox, the best photographer we ever had in this country." (NHCHS)

the crusade for beautification was led by George Dudley Seymour. It was Seymour's dream to create a ring of parkland around the city, with parkways providing radial access. These parkways, with planted grassy center strips, would also serve to bring the parks into the inner city, and every resident was to have one within a block or two of his home. A few were constructed and portions are visible today in Norton Parkway, Edgewood Parkway, Tower Parkway, and Saltonstall Parkway. A substantial addition to the city parkland was achieved by George Dudley Seymour who enlisted the assistance of his friend, President William Howard Taft, to acquire Fort Hale and Lighthouse parks. Seymour inspired park and city planning continuing to this day, and was responsible for the preservaton of the Green, the restoration of the Congregational churches, the building of the post office, library, and Union Trust buildings in a classical style, the appointment of a city superintendent of trees, various traffic flow improvements, the opening of cultural facilities on Sunday afternoons, as well as the partial development of the outer ring of parks. In all of his efforts Seymour emphasized that it was not mere esthetics, but the utility of social planning which motivated him, for:

When all citizens . . . feel that they can enjoy, not by suffrance, but as a matter of right, such privileges as the place affords, then the citizens will begin to participate, not merely in the privileges, but in the obligations of the community, and many of our perplexing problems of municipal government will have disappeared.

Social planning involved the inner person as well as his surroundings, and proper health care was valued in New Haven from the days of founding. The first midwife, Hannah Beecher, received the town's gratitude and recognition when they paid for the repair and upkeep of her property. Doctors, too, appeared early in New Haven history, but except for pesthouses used during epidemics, there was no hospital until 1826–27. At that time the oldest institution for the care of the ill in Connecticut, the Connecticut State Hospital, was established, which was later named the New Haven Hospital. In 1873, a training school for nurses was established by Georgeanna Woolsey Bacon, one of the first to be developed according to Florence Nightingale's principles.

The care of the mentally ill was decided in an early city ordinance of 1791 which provided for the construction of a workhouse. To this multipurpose institution were consigned all "petty criminals, beggars, insane persons, and both vicious and virtuous paupers." Through the combined efforts of Dorothea Dix and Benjamin Silliman, this practice was terminated in 1849 when mental disorders first began to be treated as an illness. In 1908 the pioneer So-

ciety for Mental Hygiene was founded in New Haven by Clifford Beers, a young Yale graduate, whose dramatic autobiography, *A Mind That Found Itself*, provided the impetus.

The care of orphans was managed mainly by women. In 1833 an asylum was founded by The New Haven Female Society for the Relief of Orphans, Half-Orphans, and Destitute Children. A Catholic orphan asylum was founded in 1865. Another early women's project was the Home for the Friendless, which cared for destitute wives with small children, women in poor health, and elderly women without means. To provide safe, comfortable housing for the many young women coming to work in the city, as well as meaningful leisure-time activities, the Young Women's Christian Association was organized in 1880. Its first home was acquired on Chapel Street at Wooster Square. In 1891, the YWCA founded the Women's Exchange whereby middleclass women could exchange goods or services for monetary profit and remain anonymous.

The New Haven Orphan Asylum's first home was this small cottage on Grove Street, purchased through the generosity of Dr. Jonathan Knight. Knight's action was taken after Mrs. Daniels, a widow, pleaded with him and the Reverend Harry Croswell not to send her children to the almshouse. (NHCHS)

Immigrants found steady employment on the construction crews that built the city's trolley lines. These workers were photographed as they laid track on Church Street. From the Gladding Collection, NHCHS.

Facing page
Top
The Church of the Redeemer maintained Welcome Hall on Oak Street from 1898 to 1943. This center for religious and welfare work offered programs that helped immigrant families adjust to their new surroundings. Photo by Myron W. Filley. (NHCHS)

Bottom
The Italian immigrants who came to work in New Haven's factories gravitated to the area around Wooster Square. The beauty of the square in this late 19th-century photograph belies the grueling 12 and 14 hour workdays of the people who lived around it. Photo by Myron W. Filley. (NHCHS)

Settlement houses, day-care centers, and free kindergartens began to spring up around the city to cope with the needs of the new immigrant population. Until the late 1840s, immigration had been gradual. Class distinctions and social prestige evolved from old English customs. The first major wave of immigrants came from Ireland, mainly after the potato famine. Irish were employed first in canal building, then railroad building. By the time of the Civil War, they had trained military organizations who were militarized and provided highly valued service. In 1880 Italians and Eastern Europeans began to pour into the city. Factory and construction jobs were plentiful for men, and women could usually find employment in the large corset factories or do piecework at home. The immigrant ethnic groups also organized their own social agencies, such as the Hebrew Benevolent Society and the Knights of Columbus.

By 1900, 28 percent of the city population of 100,000 was foreign-born. There seemed to be no end of growth in sight as the economy boomed and the population swelled. After World

War I restrictive anti-immigration laws drastically cut down the flow of arrivals from Europe. The new waves then came mainly from U.S. areas—blacks from the South and Hispanics from Puerto Rico. New ethnic neighborhoods emerged in the 20th century. The area around Wooster Street and Square was settled by Italians who found it convenient to walk to the large factories, especially Sargent's hardware plant. In the "Hill" section south of the downtown area, Irish and Germans were replaced by Eastern European Jews and some Italians. Oak Street and its western extension, Legion Avenue, had a European air with a multitude of small shops, sidewalk stands, and pushcarts, which were closed on the Saturday Sabbath and open Sunday. One Yale student of the Class of 1907, a Minnesotan named Sinclair Lewis, was fascinated by the Oak Street ambience and pointed out to his fellow students that "All of us can learn many things about New Haven, to our exceeding profit. How many of the Class in 'American Social Conditions' think that only New York has slums?" Ten years after leaving

New Haven the memory was given literary life in Lewis's short story, "Young Man Axelbrod":

They reached the campus at about five in the morning. . . . Policemen wondered to see the celluloid-collared old man and the expensive-looking boy rolling arm in arm down Chapel Street in search of a restaurant suitable to poets. They were all closed.

"The Ghetto will be awake by now," said Gil. "We'll go buy some eats and take 'em up to my room. . . ."

Down on Oak Street, a place of low shops, smoky lights and alley mouths, they found the slum already astir. Gil contrived to purchase boxed biscuits, cream cheese, chicken-loaf, a bottle of cream. While Gil was chaffering, Knute stared out into the street milkily lighted by wavering gas and the first feebleness of coming day; he gazed upon Kosher signs and advertisements in Russian letters, shawled women and bearded rabbis; and as he looked he gathered contentment which he could never lose. He had traveled abroad tonight.

When the Depression of 1929 struck, New Haven suffered, but the blow was softened by the massive building pro-

gram that Yale University embarked upon in the late 1920s. With the unprecedented bequest of John William Sterling and the generous donations of Edward S. Harkness, Yale built residential colleges, professional schools, and the monumental Sterling Memorial Library. The library alone employed the skills of some 300 construction workers, mostly Italians, and 1,200 men in all worked on the Yale buildings that rose on many city streets. By 1938, the Tercentenary Year, the population of the city reached 163,000, with a regional population of 300,000. The highlight of the celebration was the Pageant presented in the Yale Bowl with a cast of thousands of city residents. Among the 23 scenes was a tribute to New Haven as the melting pot of nations. Yale alumni poet, Stephen Vincent Benet, wrote the Tercentenary Ode, which included among its 10 stanzas the following lines:

And the vision of something greater, not yet built on the earth. It has flickered and changed and altered with time and the changing years,

War work carried New Haven through the late 1930s and mid-1940s. Thereafter, the changing economy and exodus to the suburbs left the city in a depressed condition. The major characteristics which had determined New Haven's early greatness now seemed to many to have caused its postwar deterioration. The encouragement of educational and religious organizations by granting tax-free status, and the loss of its outlying towns when the city incorporated in 1784, meant that New Haven no longer had a large enough tax base to provide needed so-

cial services. The census of 1970 revealed that the population had shrunk to 137,000. A study by "Goals for New Haven," a non-profit agency, defined seven problem areas that faced the city in the '70s:

1. A population loss of 34,000 from 1950 to 1970 that was disproportionately high in upper- and middle-income groups.
2. The job loss due to the movement of factories away from the city and slowdown in opening new ones.
3. A shrinking tax base caused by job and population movement out of the city, leaving reduced funds to pay for social services needed by the increasingly poor population.
4. Social unrest and racial tension maximized by state and federal welfare policies that kept residents "locked in" blighted neighborhoods.
5. Crime and the fear of crime that minimize city efforts to lure back the middle class.
6. The decline in the quality of education, which stimulates migration and the favoring of private schools.
7. Abandonment of housing caused by the inability to secure loans and fire insurance.

At the same time, Goals for New Haven noted opportunities for civic improvement within the problem areas: the change in population mix would encourage middle-class couples, especially when both spouses work, to buy houses in the city, and the elderly to rent apartments; the drop in school-age population would decrease education costs and the crime rate; unused school

facilities could be converted to other uses; other vacant facilities and land owned by the city could be used to attract new enterprises; and as some neighborhoods thin out, the cost of providing city services to those areas would decline correspondingly.

As New Haven approached the 340th anniversary of its birth, some positive and optimistic signs of faith in its regeneration were evident. Speeches and reports affirmed that the city was "turning around." Instead of a monolithic redevelopment program, rebirth concentrated on neighborhood preservation and urban homesteading. It seemed now that the city could be revitalized by building on its social diversity, rather than on a decaying unity. The special roots of New Haven's past were recognized in the city's celebration of the national Bicentennial.

New historical societies were founded and flourished alongside the New Haven Colony Historical Society, including the Afro-American Historical Society, the Jewish Historical Society, the Italian Historical Society, the Irish History Round Table, and the Fair Haven Preservation and Historical Society. Perhaps the vision of what New Haven could be, as described by Isaac Ullman in an earlier critical period, would at last be realized. In his first report as President of the New Haven Chamber of Commerce in 1910, Ullman declared that "New Haven shall not only be known as the 'City of Elms,' but as the city of good schools, the city of good health, the city of ample police and fire protection, the city of well-paved and well-lighted streets, the city clean and the 'City Beautiful.'"

The drive along the shore of Fort Hale had only recently been lined with saplings when George Edmondson photographed it about 1890. (NHCHS)

111

Despite an occasional violent confrontation, the relationship between town and gown has most often resembled the scene in this 1856 engraving. Yale students playing ball near the State House coexist in peace with citizens strolling on the Green. From the Dana Collection, NHCHS.

TABLE OF SIGNIFICANT DATES IN NEW HAVEN SOCIAL HISTORY

1638	Quinnipiac Indians settle in reservation on East Shore.
1717	First Italian immigrant settles in New Haven; William Diodate of Genoa.
1754	A ship arrives bearing 38 Irish servants.
1757	Ezra Stiles records the presence of five Acadian families.
1772	Stiles records that a family of Venetian Jews settled in New Haven.
1774	Black population recorded at 273.
1811	First black school opened.
1818	New state constitution states that "no preference shall be given by law to any Christian sect or mode of worship."
1820	First black congregation, the Congregational "United African Society," established with the help of Simeon Jocelyn.
1824	Construction of Farmington Canal brings Irish to New Haven.
1826/27	New Haven Hospital organized.
1832	Catholic Church established.
1836	First black minister installed; the Reverend J. W. C. Pennington.
1839	Railroad begins operation between New Haven and Meriden, and reaches Hartford in 1840.
1840	Bavarian Jews organize first Jewish congregation.
1843	State of Connecticut amends statutes to permit Jews to form a congregation.
1845	Potato famine in Ireland starts large wave of immigration to New Haven.
1848	Sigismond Waterman of New Haven, a German instructor at Yale, becomes first Jewish graduate of Yale, receiving the M.D. degree.
1848	First use of gaslight.
1857	First known Irish alderman.
1858	First German-Catholic church established.
1861	Thomas S. Cahill of New Haven commands the Connecticut Irish Regiment that

	includes 250 New Haveners.
1865	First Lutheran church organized by German immigrants.
1868	German Baptists organize a church.
1873	New Haven ceases to be a co-capital of Connecticut.
1876	First black graduate of Yale, Edward Bouchet, Class of 1874, is awarded Yale Ph.D., the first earned by a black person in America.
1880	Italian population reaches 500.
1881	Second wave of Jewish immigration from Eastern Europe begins.
1882	Knights of Columbus organize.
1882	Swedish Baptist church established.
1883	Swedish Lutheran church established.
1883	Polish community begins with settlement of five families.
1888	Italian community reaches 2,000 and establishes first church, St. Michaels.
1889	French-Canadians establish St. Louis church.
1889	First Ukranian settlement.
1892	Sylvester and Joseph Poli open the first of their theaters.
1892	First Columbus Day festivities held on 400th anniversary of discovery of America; Fund raised to erect Columbus monument on Wooster Square.
1892	Calvary Baptist Church starts voluntary work with local Chinese residents.
1893	Electricity utilized to power streetlights and streetcars.

1895	Lithuanians form the St. Francis Beneficial Society.
1895	First Greek businessman, Christos Koutsoheris, begins work.
1899	First immigrant elected mayor, Cornelius R. Driscoll, an Irishman.
1901	Polish church, St. Stanislaus, is founded.
1908	Lithuanian community is granted parish status by Bishop.
1910	Italians surpass Irish as largest foreign-born ethnic group.
1910	Report of the City Improvement Commission by Cass Gilbert and Frederic Law Olmstead, Jr., is published.
1914	Yale Bowl completed.
1917	First Jewish mayor, Samuel Campner, president of Board of Aldermen, is appointed to fill out term of Mayor Rice.
1924	First Greek Orthodox church built.
1927	Opening of New Haven airport.
1934/35	Hispanic community first established with settlement of seven Puerto Rican men.
1938	300th Anniversary of the founding celebrated.
1946	First mayor of Italian descent, William C. Celentano.
1950	Levi Jackson of New Haven elected first black captain of Yale football team.
1951	Ukrainian Orthodox church organized.
1972	Construction begins on first church building for Spanish-speaking residents.

MOULTHROP & LITCHS'

GREAT SKY LIGHT GALLERY OF
DAGUERREOTYPES,

NOS. 23 & 24 PHŒNIX BUILDING, CHAPEL ST., NEW HAVEN.

The subscribers would respectfully inform their friends that they have perfected their **SKY-LIGHT** arrangements for taking Daguerreotype Likenesses in the most superior style of this highly interesting and useful art. In addition to their very large and superior sett of **GERMAN VOITLANDER CAMERAS,** they have discovered a new and simple way of subduing the intensity of light upon their sitters, rendering it more agreeable to their eyes than heretofore, and, as a consequence, giving a much more truthful and pleasing resemblance to their pictures.

Success in this Art requires greater personal skill and artistic taste than the unthinking public generally suppose; in fact, more than nine-tenths of the Daguerreotypists imagine, and we see, as a natural result, that while the business numbers its thousands of votaries, but few rise to any degree of eminence. We do not wish to claim any thing more than is DUE to ourselves as operators, but at the same time, it is proper that the public should know that no firm of this kind has the advantage of us in experience, that we know of in the United States, one of the firm having been in the business eleven years and the other nearly eight, and previous to this about twelve years engaged in Drawing and Painting, thus giving us a good degree of experience so essentially necessary in the composition of groups, in the combination of chemicals, attitudes, and especially in the arrangement of light and shade upon our sitters.

For the benefit of those who have any misgivings about the durability of Daguerreotype Miniatures, we would state that it is the opinion of the most scientific men in this country, that if WELL FINISHED, they will stand the test of age.

MINIATURES inserted in Lockets, Pins, Rings, Bracelets, &c. in the neatest style, and at greatly reduced prices, and to the satisfaction of all who may favor us with their patronage. American and German Apparatus, Plates, Chemicals, Cases, Frames, Lockets, &c. on hand, and forwarded to order. Instruction in all branches of the Art.
Portraits, Engravings, and Daguerreotypes Neatly Copied.

Chapter VII
THE ARTS IN NEW HAVEN
by Reverdy Whitlock

Photographic studios multiplied in New Haven, as they did in other cities, after the Civil War, and local artists suffered the consequences. Artist Major Moulthrop decided to fight fire with fire. His first "daguerrean rooms" opened for business in 1845. Moulthrop remained an active photographer until his death in 1890. (NHCHS)

A pundit said once that in Boston, Cabots speak only to Lowells and Lowells speak only to God, while in New Haven the deity converses with Jones in the very same tones he uses with Hadley and Dwight.

There is more than a vein of truth in these observations. Their origins, not so old perhaps as Mr. Winthrop's fleet that brought his first settlers to Massachusetts in 1630, or Mr. Davenport's sermon in Mr. Newman's barn, still are hidden in the mists of time. What is said is simply that New Haven never quite belonged to the world of Anne Bradstreet and Cotton Mather, nor to the galaxy of bearded and beatific poets—those 19th-century worthies, Bryant and Whittier, Lowell and Longfellow—to whom, Van Wyck Brooks used to say, New England owed her flowering.

New Haven, caught in the gravitational pull of Boston, that bastion of Puritan orthodoxy, on the one hand, and of New York and the hedonistic and secular world that lay beyond, on the other, quite early decided that it would belong to neither. And so it was that here, despite the entreaties of John Davenport and, much later, of Leonard Bacon, the rigors of Calvinism were much softened, just as the biting cold of New England winters yielded to the warming influences of Long Island Sound.

The town had its beginnings in the Puritan exodus, when a mixture of religious and economic motives brought to New England, as John Milton put it, "faithful and freeborn Englishmen and good Christians constrained to forsake their dearest home, their friends and kindred, whom nothing but the wide ocean and the savage deserts of America could hide and shelter from the fury of the bishops." These were Englishmen and they brought with them the English language, English architecture, English ideas of jurisprudence, English political institutions, English concepts of town and family organization, and views of the world and their place in it which were peculiarly English. Who can say when these hardy yeomen no longer thought of themselves as Englishmen, and when a native American culture molded by the American wilderness emerged as a dominant theme in the life of the colonies? It came slowly, as the founding fathers were laid in their graves and the end of the pilgrim century made way for a new generation of colonials who had never seen the busy streets of London or the rolling Cotswold hills.

The settlement at Quinnipiac, deeply rooted in the cultural heritage of western Europe, would in time assume cultural patterns of its own. Rid of the panoply and splendor of the established Church of England under

115

Archbishop Laud, John Davenport in New Haven and John Cotton in Boston proceeded to mold a new orthodoxy in New England, quite as intolerant of dissent as the old had been. So inflexible were the rules that required support of what Cotton Mather called the "New English churches," that it was not until 1727 when the Episcopalians—followed by the Quakers in 1729—were exempted from them.

In 1674 James Fitch, the first minister in Norwich and a ranking member of the clerical elite, preached the Connecticut colony's election sermon. In it he recalled the Golden Age: "Let us call to minde the first glory in the first planting of New England and of the Churches here. Let us say multitudes, multitudes were converted to thee, O Hartford, to thee, O New Haven, to thee, O Windsor!"

The rule of the churches in the New England church-state would be challenged by forces—political, social, and economic—which at last would bring about its downfall.

It must be recalled that for a very long time New Haven remained almost wholly white, Anglo-Saxon, and Protestant. This homogeneous society, transplanted to Massachusetts Bay and almost simultaneously to Connecticut, was sustained until well into the 19th century. In the 1830s it would be influenced by the Irish exodus accelerated by the potato famines, and by later infusions of Germans fleeing the political upheavals in Germany after 1848, and by emigrants escaping the social and economic unrest in Italy and Russia later in the century. The dramatic impact of these pre-World War I population shifts was followed after 1941 by a large in-migration of blacks, largely agrarian, seeking a better life in the industrial cities of the north.

Culture is hard to define. In a sense it is an amalgam of thoughts and feelings, of ideas and institutions, of manners and traditions, and of creative skills finding their articulation in the arts. The cultural historian wants to know why Jonathan Edwards said what he did about infant damnation and the Half-Way Covenant and how Donald Grant Mitchell's farm at Edgewood was related to the new urbanism. Cultural history sees these phenomena in relation to the political, social, and economic circumstances out of which they have sprung and of which they are a part. It is more concerned with the murals on post-office walls occasioned by the stock market crash in the autumn of 1929 than with the economic debacle itself. The dimity convictions of the small world of Amherst, Massachusetts, flourished in the arid soil of Puritanism, but it is Emily Dickinson's response to them that is the stuff of the student of culture.

The cultural history of New Haven is a bit like a tapestry, in which the basic design takes its form from the life of the 17th-century English yeoman class, embellished by an overlay of other elements woven later into it. The newer ethnic groups have added much color and richness to the cultural fabric of the town founded by those venturesome bands of freeborn Englishmen under Davenport and Eaton.

And so in New Haven we must concern ourselves with the growth of artistic expression through the first flowerings of the Puritan commonwealth, on into the 18th century with its growing wealth and secularism, and the 19th when it was the handmaiden of the new industrialism and the laissez-faire economics of the Gilded Age. And finally we must reckon with the return to primitivism early in our own century under the aegis of William Morris and Elbert Hubbard, followed by the Gothic revival of James Gamble Rogers and the alabaster splendor of the City Beautiful as it emerged full-blown from the fertile fancies of George Dudley Seymour.

The earliest settlements along the coast and river lines were transplanted English villages. Prototypes of New Haven's central square or Green might be seen all over England and the dwellings which surrounded it were clearly derivative. The wood-framed struc-

tures of Essex and the home counties seem to have inspired the basic architectural themes in the New World, where the first buildings were thatched and half-timbered in the Elizabethan style. Before the end of the first century of colonization and by a sort of Darwinian process of selection, many features of English architecture were discarded in favor of building styles and techniques more suited to Connecticut.

Since the separation of church and state would not be clearly defined until the passage of the new constitution in 1818, it is not surprising that the first public structure in New Haven was a meetinghouse. This primitive building was replaced in the 1660s by a more commodious one, which in turn would make way in 1756 for a third, a side-entrance meetinghouse with the pulpit on the long axis.

While these three meetinghouses were the earliest public buildings, there were others. Opened in 1718 to provide quarters for the Collegiate School, the building known as Yale College in honor of its principal benefactor Elihu Yale would be the infant institution's only structure until mid-century. In 1750 Yale's architectural resources were augmented with the erection of Connecticut Hall followed in 1761 by the

Georgian first chapel (later the Atheneum) just south of it. Then in 1793 came South College to be followed by North Middle College in 1801, the Lyceum in 1803, North College in 1820, and Divinity College in 1835. These were the buildings that formed the Old Brick Row of blessed memory. Symbols in brick and mortar of Yale's presence in the town, they were for so long an ingredient in the cultural climate that they became part of the community subconscious. And then they were gone—with the exception of Connecticut Hall—victims of the grand design of Timothy Dwight the Younger for an unbroken phalanx of buildings around the college square.

While New Haven had hosted the October sessions of the General Assembly since 1701, sharing with Hartford the honor of being co-capital of the colony, it did not have its own statehouse until 1719. That year saw the erection of a handsome new structure embellishing the northwest corner of the Green. Growing in opulence as the 18th century moved on, the colony put up a handsome new Georgian building near Chapel and Temple streets in 1763 to replace the old one. Then came Ithiel Town in 1828 with his grand neoclassic edifice, designed after the Temple of Theseus at Athens and des-

The sloping lawn and warm red color of Yale's Old Brick Row linked the college to the fabric of the city that surrounded it when this photograph was taken circa 1860. (NHCHS)

Top
Henry Austin designed Yale's Old Library in the Gothic style. It could be viewed in the same way as the English country chapels that inspired it before buildings covered the surrounding land in the 20th century (NHCHS)

Right
Ernest Machado's plan for a civic group on Elm Street included a public library, county courthouse, and hall of records. Firm support for the plan on the part of George Dudley Seymour failed to win its adoption by the city council. From the Seymour Collection, NHCHS.

Below
Daniel Read (1757-1841) served as choir leader and organist of the United Society on the Green. He wrote and published The American Singing Book, An Introduction to Psalmody *and* The Columbian. *He also created* The American Musical Magazine, *which appeared monthly and consisted of works by American and European composers. (NHCHS)*

tined to grace the upper Green until its untimely destruction in 1889. That New Haven should be called the Athens of the New World is both hyperbolic and understandable.

Town, renowned for his truss bridge and for his Federal design for the new meetinghouse completed for the First Society in 1814, was responsible as well for the avant-garde Gothic scheme for Trinity Church just south of it.

Equally versatile was Henry Austin, who had been commissioned by Yale to create a Gothic plan for the new Yale Library of 1842, and who moved on to a profusion of Italianate dwellings for the haute bourgeoisie as the century progressed toward the Gilded

Age. His crowning achievement was the Ruskinesque City Hall, dedicated in 1862. Conceived in the grand manner, with a central atrium reaching up to the very top of the building and a skylight to illumine a palatial iron stairway, the new City Hall became a powerful symbol of urban pride expressed in a new and daring architectural idiom.

After 1900 would come Cass Gilbert, fulfilling George Dudley Seymour's prophecies of new urban grandeur with his design for the Ives Memorial Library in 1911 and Union Station in 1918. These soaring fantasies were embodied in a master plan for the "City Beautiful," a new heaven and a new earth right here in this other Eden.

on the banks of the Quinnipiac. If the utopian schemes of George Dudley Seymour have somehow got lost in the shuffle, it does not follow of necessity that they lack validity. It can be argued that like Bronson Alcott's Fruitlands and the idea of a Christian society, they have not really been tried.

After the Old Brick Row was gone and the Yale Fence along with it, in the bicentennial year the Woolsey Hall complex would clearly show that what the retiring younger Dwight had found in brick, he intended to leave in stone. Two decades later a new frenzy of building, inaugurated with James Gamble Rogers's Harkness Memorial Quadrangle in 1917, was followed by the Sterling Memorial Library, the Sterling Law Buildings, the Payne Whitney Gymnasium, and a plethora of new colleges and classrooms.

Yale's metamorphosis would go on long after the demise of neo-Gothic and neo-Georgian. Louis Kahn's new Art Gallery (1953), followed by the three Eero Saarinen buildings—the Ingalls Rink (1957) and Morse and Stiles colleges (1960)—symbolized the shift away from traditional architectural forms.

Not all the new buildings belonged to Yale. Douglas Orr, who had a deft hand with Art Deco and the new Georgian, gained a measure of immortality for himself by designing a handsome new building on Church Street for the Southern New England Telephone Company.

Mayor Richard C. Lee, driven by the vision of a renewed downtown New Haven in the '50s and '60s, was to create with bold strokes a Model City. Where blight and decay had followed in the wake of the suburban exodus after World War II, would rise new urban housing, most of it supported by federal subsidies. If the vision of the brave new urban world of the 1950s was somehow to lose its luster in the 1980s, it was not because Dick Lee and his planners didn't try. They did. But it would take more than good intentions and massive infusions of federal monies to make the new ala-baster city a reality.

Dublin was built in the 18th century, as was a large part of downtown New Haven. Dublin remains today a Georgian city with a delightful homogeneity. New Haven, reflecting the restless energies of a mobile society without a clear understanding of its own life in time, has traditionally seemed less concerned with bringing together harmoniously the elements of its townscape; but with the formation of the New Haven Preservation Trust in 1962 the town has become increasingly aware of its rich and varied architectural heritage.

Music as an art form in New England had its beginnings in Calvinism. It should be recalled that the Bay Psalm Book which came off the press of Stephen Daye in Cambridge (Massachusetts) in 1640 contained no musical notation. It was designed to provide the words around which each congregation could devise and embroider its own musical interpretations. As time went on, "singing by rule," that is, with musical notation, became more and more the accepted usage. Making a joyful noise unto the Lord, popular belief to the contrary, was an accepted part of formal worship in the Puritan churches from the beginning. It was not until the 19th century that music would detach itself from its church origins and assert its secularity.

It could hardly be said, however, that the celebration of the life of the community through music was a dominant 19th-century theme. After the Civil War, New Haven's energies were largely given to the accumulation of private wealth and to the construction of new streets and the buildings that lined them. The blatant materialism of the age of the robber barons did not give much more than self-conscious and symbolic encouragement to the arts. The experience of art, it must be said, was often little more than a polite affectation.

Yale, always a strong presence in the affairs of the town, played an important part in the evolution of New

Haven's musical activities from the middle of the century on. A Yale Beethoven Society was formed in 1850 and in 1869 the Yale Glee Club regaled the community with vocal music, for the first time without formal church ties. It was clear after the war that secular music would soon enjoy a life of its own.

But for an unfortunate occurrence, New Haven might have had its own symphonic orchestra long before the New Haven Symphony gave its first concert in Yale's Alumni Hall on Thursday, March 14, 1895. An embryonic symphonic group had been put together in the '60s by Morris Steinert, born in Bavaria in 1831, who had come to America a decade earlier, quite appropriately in the sailing ship *Jenny Lind.* The Steinert Orchestra, as it was called, had got off to an auspicious start when the Young Men's Institute engaged it to play before each of a series of weekly lectures. Then came the fateful evening in the late '60s when it was slated to render a few appropriate selections at a temperance lecture in the old Bunnell Opera House. It seems regrettable that the lecture on the evils of strong drink coincided with the birthday of one of the musicians, a hapless viol player known to us only as Fischer. The Steinert Orchestra, after several hours of bacchanalian celebration of Fischer's nativity, adjourned to Mr. Bunnell's Opera House in a state of alcoholic euphoria. Despite some apprehensions of impending disaster, Mr. Steinert, quite unreasonably as it turned out, took the view that all would be well. The coup de grace came when one of the viol players, reduced to a state of total insensibility, collapsed on stage with his instrument on top of him. With this unhappy accident the soirée musicale ended. The effort failed and it would take 25 years to get a symphonic group going again.

The long twilight ended in March 1895 when a new symphony orchestra, under the direction of the immortal Horatio Parker and featuring the works of Edward Grieg and Max Bruch, played to a packed audience who had paid 25 cents each for the privilege of being there. It was, in a way, an epoch-making event but obviously far removed from the New Haven Symphony's present $1.8 million annual budget. Despite the befuddled fiddler, the New Haven Symphony Orchestra offers a current series of enchanted evenings in Woolsey Hall, a summer series of concerts on the Green, and a sparkling one at Christmas.

It would be hard, early in the century, to establish separate identities for the Neighborhood Music School and St. Paul's Church, Wooster Square. With perhaps, at first, a slight accent of *nouveau arrivisme,* the Square had nonetheless remained through most of the 19th century a bastion of Anglo-Saxon orthodoxy.

The flood of Italian immigration, starting in the 1880s, had by 1910 drawn to the Wooster Square area thousands of Italians eager to work nearby at Sargent's or the New Haven Clock Company. The First Baptist Church and the Davenport Congregational Church, yielding to ethnic pressures, decided to leave the Square. St. Paul's, under the leadership of the Reverend George Paine, embarked upon missions of service and mercy right where it was and had been from the beginning. There, at the corner of Chapel and Olive streets, began a vigorous interaction between St. Paul's and the neighborhood which has gone on ever since. There were English classes for the Italians; there were a savings bank and a circulating library. But most important there was a music school under the direction of Susan Hart Dyer and later of Jessie Clarke Beecher. It was all very warm and loving and out of it came the Neighborhood Music School, which in 1943 began its own separate corporate existence—a visible and audible symbol of the common language of music—miraculously endowed with charms transcending the barriers of race and creed. The years have not dimmed the vision of a shared community of music,

and the Neighborhood Music School, now at 100 Audubon Street, continues there its labor of love.

We cannot think about the cultural life of the community without thinking of books and newspapers. On February 5, 1793, the Mechanic Library Society met for the first time in the old State House on the Green. The decision made there to put together a collection of books was so successful that when the Library Society issued a printed list of the books on its shelves in 1801, it could boast a total of 700 volumes. These efforts to form a public repository for books did indeed lead to the birth of a quasi-public library before 1800, but it should also be said that this was by no means the first library in the town. Yale College had brought with it a collection of books when it came to New Haven in 1718.

Not satisfied with the achievements of the Mechanic Library Society, a second library got under way in 1810 with the formation of the Social Library Company, whose constitution provided that "no novels, romances, tales or plays shall be admitted into the library unless by vote of two thirds of members present at any legal meeting." With 2,000 books on its shelves in 1833, the Social Library attracted the attention of a group of young working men, banded together in 1826 for self-improvement under the formidable title "The Apprentices Literary Association," destined to become the Young Mechanic's Institute in 1828 and the New Haven Young Men's Institute in 1841. On August 5, 1840, it possessed a subscription library of 3,500 volumes, many of them acquired by purchase from the moribund Social Library Company. After a series of moves, including occupancy of the Old State House in 1875–1877, it settled in, as the Institute Library, for a good long stay at 847 Chapel Street, where it still remains, an oasis of almost monastic repose safely withdrawn from the tumultuous marketplace that surrounds it. It would be late in the 19th century before the political leadership of the town began to think about appropriations for a publicly funded free library.

Following an authorization in 1886 by the State of Connecticut to permit New Haven to issue $100,000 in bonds for the construction of a new library building, the New Haven Public Library began its long and useful career in 1887. In February of that year the library was opened, on the second floor of the Tradesmen's Bank on Chapel Street. Before the year was out, New Haven had created the fifth largest library in America. The city fathers realized that soon more space would be needed. They bought the third Congregational Church building on Church Street and there (the present site of the Colonial Bank) the New Haven Free Public Library opened its doors in 1891.

In this golden age of private philanthropy, what benefaction could offer more rewards, in this world or the next, than that font of learning—the library? And so in 1906 Mrs. Hoadley (Mary E.) Ives turned over to the city the princely sum of $350,000 to build one. Designed by Cass Gilbert in the Colonial Revival style, it became a monument not only to Mrs. Ives but also to the flourishing city, its dreams of glory fanned to a feverish heat by George Dudley Seymour and his coterie of urbanists.

It could hardly be expected that New Haven, from the beginning a Puritan commonwealth, would give encouragement to players, strolling or stationary. The dissenters who had founded the colony were committed to the suppression of the theatre. Added to the Puritan taboos condemning the lewdness of plays and players, were the rigors of life in the wilderness, which left little time for frivolity.

The annual exhibitions of tragedies, farces, and comedies presented at Yale by the Linonian Society and later by the Brothers in Unity, must be New Haven's earliest dramatic presentations. Timothy Dwight the elder was an undergraduate actor for the Linonian Society during his four years at Yale (1765–1769), and in 1772 Linonian's

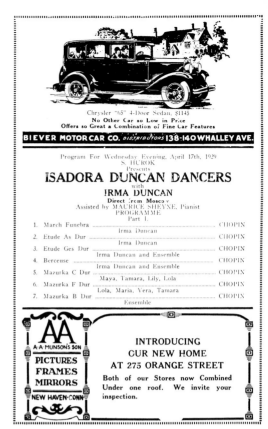

Right
Shubert Theater program, 1929. Annie Get Your Gun and South Pacific are two of the many Broadway shows that premiered at the Shubert Theater on College Street. The Isadora Duncan Dancers played the Shubert in 1929. (NHCHS)

Facing page
Top
Bunnell's Grand Opera House illustrated an 1870 advertisement for builder A. Holt. Originally called the Music Hall, it was built by Samuel Peck with proceeds from his daguerreotype-case factory on Day Street. (NHCHS)

Bottom
The price of admission to The Birth of a Nation at the Hyperion Theater included a dutiful wave for the camera from these schoolboys in 1914. Photo by T. S. Bronson. (NHCHS)

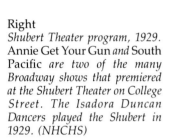

play was *The Beaux' Stratagem* performed by the martyr spy, Nathan Hale, and the planter of the elms on the Green, James Hillhouse.

Although the first recorded professional theatrical production in New Haven was staged on April 3, 1800, half a century passed before New Haven expanded its dramatic activities beyond the narrow confines of the Yale dramatic societies and similar entertainments supplied by the Lancastrian School in the basement of the Methodist Church at the northwest corner of the Green.

Then in 1848 a troupe of Negro minstrels billed as the "Apollonians" visited the city, followed in the winter and spring of 1853 by a series of plays presented in Temple Hall at the corner of Court and Orange streets by the George Wyatt Company. That eventful year saw also the opening of the first permanent theater in New Haven, Elisha Homan's Atheneum housed in Exchange Hall at Church and Chapel streets. The first performance there was followed a few weeks later by the opening of Wyatt's Dramatic Lyceum

in Temple Hall. Then followed the unhappy demise of two theaters, opened in 1855. Doomed to early failures were the American Theatre, Church and Crown streets, and the Union Theatre in Union Hall, Union Street. At mid-century, New Haven was not yet ready to support large theatrical enterprises. By 1884 the ancient shibboleths were breaking down. In that year the master showman, G. P. Bunnell, leased the Grand Opera House, which had made its debut with a concert by the New York Philharmonic Society on November 19, 1860. It would be called Bunnell's Grand Opera House and it would provide vigorous competition for Carl's Opera House, which had opened in 1880 with 2,000 seats.

By 1900, Poli's Theatre and the Hyperion were featuring vaudeville attractions. Soon advancing technology would impose on the town the antics of the Keystone Kops, the bewitching charms of Lillian Gish, and the mass hysterias of the many-periled Pauline. The age of the film was at hand, bringing with it a half dozen baroque movie palaces designed to provide escape

from the harsh realities of a competitive laissez-faire economy and the stern dictates of the work ethic. Through the magic doors of Mr. Poli's Bijou and its competitors passed the multitudes seeking solace in this new world of the celluloid dream factories. Not until the suburban exodus following World War II and the advent of television would their spell be broken.

A joy for small children, a diversion for their parents on Sunday afternoons, an occupation for scholars and a preoccupation for all of New Haven, the Peabody Museum has been part of the community consciousness since it opened in 1876.

On October 22, 1866, George Peabody gave to Yale the princely sum of $150,000 "for foundation and maintenance of a Museum of Natural History, especially of Departments of Zoology, Geology and Mineralogy in connection with Yale College." A group of trustees designated $100,000 for a building, $20,000 for a building fund, and $30,-000 for maintenance. These sums were augmented by a Peabody son-in-law, Othniel Charles Marsh, who donated

The PRODIGAL SON revelling with HARLOTS
He wasted his Substance with Riotious Living.
St Luke 15 Chap. 13 V.
Published and Sold by Shelton & Kensett, Cheshire Con. October 31, 1814.

a large part of his estate for the building of the Peabody Museum collections before his death in 1899.

Not content with permanent occupancy of the first museum at the corner of Elm and High streets, Anson Phelps Stokes opened negotiations in 1905 for purchase of the 33-acre Hillhouse estate, enough to provide plenty of room for museum expansion. The Yale Corporation with the ebullience which characterized those last days before the income tax, at last bought the property with a $650,000 gift it had just received from Mrs. Russell Sage. That august body, with the same prodigality which had a decade earlier torn down the Old Brick Row, gave its *nihil obstat* to the destruction of the old Peabody Museum. It knew that Mrs. Stephen Vincent Harkness had the funds ready for the great Gothic memorial to her son, Charles William Harkness, B.A. 1883. The new buildings would fit nicely on the Peabody site. In 1917, that year of America's entry into the European holocaust, the Yale Corporation voted to demolish the old building. Down it went that summer, just in time for the laying of the cornerstone of the Memorial Quadrangle on October 8, 1917.

The Corporation, which had been in a compulsive hurry to get the site ready, then had to put the collections into mothballs while it looked around for someone who could grace the newly ought land in the Hillhouse quarter with a museum complex. The architect, Charles Z. Klauder, designed it and had it ready for inspection on Alumni Day, February 23, 1924. When it was all done, the people of the town would marvel at Mr. Marsh's fossils, not the least of which were the Odontornithes, the massive toothed birds magnificently laid out for all to see.

New Haven has been a literary place from the beginning. Even before John Davenport's house was built at the corner of State and Elm streets, he had written *A Discourse about Civil Government in a new Plantation whose Design is Religion*, which was published in Cambridge by Samuel Green and Marmaduke Johnson three years after the author's death in 1670.

While he was teaching school in the 17th-century schoolhouse on the Green, Ezekiel Cheever, the town's first schoolmaster, had turned out a treatise on Latin called *A Short Introduction to the Latin Tongue.*

The most elequent spokesman for the rigorous tenets of Calvinism was Michael Wigglesworth. Arriving here with his parents in the year of the planting of the colony, 1638, he would later instill terror in the hearts of the godly and the godless alike with his polemic, *The Day of Doom; or a Poetical Discription of the Great and Last Judgment with a Short Discourse about Eternity.* The rolling thunder of this work—the quintessential expression of the Calvinist dialectic—was employed for one purpose. It was to bring sinners to repentance. And it did.

Yale's first President, Thomas Clap, wrote the *Code of Laws,* destined to become in 1755 the first book printed in New Haven. The untimely visit of the British in 1779 destroyed most of President Clap's voluminous history of Connecticut. More fortunate was Ezra Stiles, president of Yale from 1779 to his death in 1795, whose diary and bound manuscripts in the college library fill some 45 volumes. In the pantheon of Yale literary greats must be included John Trumbull, Yale 1767,

who had successfully passed the required examinations for admission to Yale at the age of seven. As a tutor at Yale, he wrote *The Progress of Dullness,* and later *McFingall,* a satire on "the follies and extravagences of my countrymen." Timothy Dwight, Yale 1769, had completed his *Conquest of Canaan* in 1774 and years later a delightful travel journal called *Travels in New England and New York,* published after his death. The father of geography, Jedidiah Morse, published his *Geography Made Easy* in 1784, followed by additional printings as the book became a staple in the curricula of schools across the country.

The career of Noah Webster, Yale 1778, must be counted among the most distinguished of the Federal era. After moving to New Haven in 1798 and serving as an alderman and a representative in the General Assembly, he began his magnum opus, the *American Dictionary of the English Language* in 1807. It was published in 1828, long after his *Elementary Spelling Book,* the famed "Blue Backed Speller," had come into common use in American schools. So popular was the spelling book, with its simple homilies and its moralistic tone, that 41,000,000 copies—an impressive number by any yardstick—had been sold before January 1862.

As the century moved on toward the Civil War in those halcyon days which Van Wyck Brooks has called the time of New England's cultural flowering, Donald Grant Mitchell emerged as a major literary figure. Writing in the didactic style of Washington Irving and with the same awareness of the passing of the simple life of the farm and village as America rushed into urbanism and the excesses of the Gilded Age, he appealed to a large audience. It is no wonder that *My Farm at Edgewood, Wet Days at Edgewood, Dream Days,* and *Reveries of a Bachelor,* with their bucolic flavor and their disdain for the evils of cities and the satanic mills they spawned, became great favorites. They made "Ik Marvel," as Mitchell called himself, quite rich and the undisputed lord of

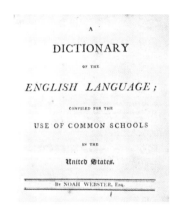

Noah Webster specifically compiled this edition of his dictionary for use in public schools. His "Blue Backed Speller" became standard reading for millions of 19th-century American schoolchildren. From the Webster Collection, NHCHS.

The Arts in New Haven
Whitlock

Top left
Bradford Hubbard was painted by East Haven artist Reuben Moulthrop circa 1790. Moulthrop's stark characterizations are powerful images despite his lack of artistic training. (NHCHS)

Top right
Nathaniel Jocelyn's 1833 portrait of Mary Oakes Hotchkiss is typical of his reserved portrait style. His dark, impenetrable backgrounds focus the viewer's attention directly on the face of the subject. (NHCHS)

Right
The Trumbull Gallery on Yale's Old Campus was the first college art museum in the United States. Windows were added when the gallery became Yale's Treasury Building in 1869. Photo by Willis N. Butricks. (NHCHS)

the manor of Edgewood, where he lived out a long life of husbandry and domestic felicity.

Painting flourished early in New Haven. Among the first flowers of the Connecticut wilderness was John Smybert, who had come to America with Bishop Berkeley in 1728. In 1750 he had painted *Dean Berkeley's Family*, which early came into the possession of Yale College.

A young aide-de-camp to General Washington, Colonel John Trumbull, son of Connecticut's revolutionary governor Jonathan Trumbull, was destined to become a sort of Boswell, commemorating in oils the battles and leaders of the Revolution. After grad-

uation from Harvard in 1773, he spent the tumultuous years 1775 and 1776 in the service of the commander-in-chief. His army career ended, he took off for London to study painting under Benjamin West. Out of this apprenticeship came a series of paintings depicting the great events of the Revolution. Late in life he executed copies of his historical paintings, some 54 in all, which he gave to Yale. That institution in turn gave the artist an annuity and allowed him to design a building in the classical style to house the paintings. When the Trumbull Gallery was opened on October 29, 1832, it became the first academically related art gallery in America. Beneath it were laid the mortal remains of Colonel Trumbull and his consort, later removed to Street Hall.

Without the gentle urgings of the New Haven born, bred, and trained portrait painter, Nathaniel Jocelyn, it seems unlikely that Yale would have established its School of Fine Arts as early as it did. It was Jocelyn who persuaded his friend, Augustus Street, Yale 1812, to give the money for a new art building. It was named Street Hall, and it would give immortality of sorts to its donor as well as creating for Yale the distinction of sponsoring the first college-related school of fine arts in America.

Quite detached from Yale, from the fashionable Hudson River painters and from the polite society of the town, was George Henry Durrie, a pupil of Jocelyn. Born in 1820, he became an itinerant portrait painter in youth, turning later to landscapes, eagerly sought after in the '50s and '60s by dwellers in cities who recalled with warmth and tenderness the life on the farms where they had grown up. It was the winter scenes especially which sustained the mood of a rural America, dissolving before men's eyes in the mid-century rush to industry and urbanism.

There were important additions to Street Hall later on. Augustus Russell Street had wanted the School of Fine Arts "to be also a source of education to the . . . people of New Haven." These contributions were enlarged in 1926 with the gift from Edward S. Harkness of money for a new gallery, and in 1953 with the building of an additional wing, designed by Louis Kahn as his first major commission.

On the south side of Chapel Street, across the way, Kahn's last building, one he was destined not to see finshed, would go up 20 years later. Founded in 1968 by Paul Mellon, Yale 1929, the Yale Center for British Art opened its doors on April 19, 1977, to house Mr. Mellon's vast collections. Among Mellon's stated objectives was the fostering of an appreciation and knowledge of British art, as well as creating facilities for a broad program of British studies.

Despite its very obvious benefactions, it does not appear that Yale's long shadow has in any measure diminished the artistic initiatives of the larger community. There are ample evidences—the Long Wharf Theatre, the Connecticut Ballet Company, the Creative Arts Workshop, and the New Haven Colony Historical Society, to name a few—that the town gets along very well on its own.

As the 20th century draws to a close, New Haven finds itself, like most American cities, the victim of sweeping changes in American society not of its own making. The suburban exodus has deprived it, through the vagaries of geographical boundaries set up centuries ago, of its God-fearing, tax-paying, and hard-working middle class. Vast population shifts have thrown on its doorstep hordes of new urban poor, ill-equipped to play self-sustaining or creative roles and dependent on the welfare system for their precarious existence. Amidst the poverty the monolithic slab of Yale's Kline Tower presides over the little world of the happy few, symbolic of the great center of learning in their midst.

And within the framework of a democratic society in these last decades of a century of wars and rumors of wars the book-binding classes at the Creative Arts Workshop are flourishing, seats in Woolsey Hall for the New Haven Symphony are hard to come by, and Yale's Beinecke Rare Book and Manuscript Library boasts a collection of incunabula the Bodleian could be proud of.

In this little world, a microcosm in a vast, mobile, and materialistic society, a happy breed of men and women carries on a long tradition of intellectual activity and artistic creativity. Its influences, like the pebble in the pond, have moved over the prairies and past the western mountains to give form and purpose to the national character.

Chapter VIII

NEW HAVEN ARCHITECTURE
by William A. Wiedersheim

Though the design of New Haven's High Victorian Gothic City Hall (built in 1868) is credited to Henry Austin, the city's leading 19th-century architect, David R. Brown, Austin's apprentice (and later partner), probably designed the awesome structure. (NHCHS)

During the first century and a quarter of its existence, the New Haven Colony had few, if any, buildings of particular architectural note. Yale's first building in New Haven, a long narrow three-story wood clapboard structure, was built at the corner of College and Chapel streets in 1717, following the design of a committee headed by Governor Saltonstall. It was an all-purpose building, housing classrooms, students, tutors, a commons, kitchen, and Yale's precious library; it was the whole college.

Between 1753 and 1757, the third and most elaborate meetinghouse of the congregation of the First Church of Christ, which had been formed 14 months after the colonists landed in 1638, was built on the New Haven Green with its axis parallel to present-day Temple Street. Several paintings of it exist, and it does not seem to have been architecturally valuable. The city's first Anglican church, built near the corner of Church and Chapel streets in 1755 with suspicious misgivings on the part of the Congregationalists, sported a tall conical tower, but otherwise it too was undistinguished. Between 1750 and 1755, Yale's Connecticut Hall was built with funds realized from a lottery, the sale of a captured French ship, and a grant from the Connecticut Assembly, under the supervision of two talented masons, Francis Letort and

Thomas Bills, and stands today on Yale's Old Campus as the university's oldest building.

Fine architecture burst on the New Haven scene at the start of the 19th century through the almost simultaneous appearance of a British-born carpenter, master-builder, and architectural designer, Peter Banner (fl. 1794–1828), a Connecticut-born master-builder and self-taught architect, David Hoadley (1774–1839), and a very gifted architect and engineer, Ithiel Town (1784–1844). As a growing commercial and college town, New Haven provided ample outlet for their talents and their energies.

Peter Banner arrived in Boston in 1794 and is known to have worked in New Haven between 1799 and about 1804, when he returned to Boston. While in New Haven, he designed and prepared a cost estimate of $2,403.78 for the second home of Yale presidents, and built it on College Street near Elm in 1799. Between 1800 and 1804 he designed and built Berkeley Hall (North Middle College) and the Connecticut Lyceum on Yale's Old Brick Row. His cost estimate for the presidents' house and drawings for it and the Connecticut Lyceum are in Yale's archives; Berkeley Hall stood until 1895 and the Connecticut Lyceum until 1901. There is no known survivor of any other buildings Peter Banner might have designed and built in New Haven. His later career in Boston was illustrious; his crowning achievement was the design and construction of Boston's Park Street Church.

David Hoadley's architectural monument is the United Church on the Green (1812–1815). While its basic design may have been borrowed, its details and proportions sprang from his sure instincts, and United Church is a New England Federal meetinghouse in its purest form. No formal drawings of it exist and many of its exquisite details

building, the "Cabinet," which was built on the Old Brick Row and stood until 1890.

Hoadley's work was, however, overshadowed by that of a friendly rival, Ithiel Town, who apprenticed under Asher Benjamin in Boston and came to New Haven around 1810. In 1812 he assumed the contract to build Center Church on the Green, the fourth occupied by the congregation of the First Church of Christ; and working from a plan supplied by Benjamin

must have been Hoadley's own, for no counterpart from which they have been copied has been found. The design of the Tontine Hotel, one of New Haven's most elegant hotels for nearly a century, and which stood on Church Street at Court facing the Green, was probably that of Ithiel Town, but David Hoadley is known to have supervised its construction. He designed and built a number of handsome New Haven homes. The John Cook and Timothy Bishop homes, stately Federal town houses on lower Elm Street, are often attributed to him, and he may have designed and built the Jonathan Mix house (1799) at 177 Elm Street, now the prestigious Graduates Club. He designed Noah Webster's New Haven home which stood at the corner of Grove and Temple Streets where Yale's Silliman College now stands. For Yale he designed in 1819 the Philosophical

which adapted and simplified the exterior elevations of St. Martin-in-the-Fields in London (James Gibbs, 1726), he created a structure that might well be called his own. Its crisp and stately interior has a shallow lath-and-plaster domed ceiling; no handsomer Federal church can be found in all New England. Town had to build Center Church directly over a few of the graves that existed on the Green, but he left the gravestones intact. The church spire, reinforced with two internal cones, was fabricated on the ground and hoisted into place with tackle and windlass within a period of two hours. As it settled into place, a cheer went up from a fascinated group of onlookers.

Concurrently Town designed the third of the three handsome churches on the Green, Trinity Episcopal, in the Gothic style, one of the first Gothic Revival structures in America. Trinity's congregation did not feel that a Puritan design would be compatible with the Anglican ritual, so Gothic was selected and the church built of locally quarried stone of a warm brown and golden hue. Since then its chancel has been extended and its interior rebuilt, fortunately without harming Town's exterior and actually improving the interior.

All three of the churches on the Green were built at the same time, during the War of 1812, and the timbers turally on a lattice truss which supported a longer span than a conventional bridge. He was able to obtain a patent on the design, and it became a standard for bridges built throughout the United States and in many places in Europe for the next 70 years. His pilot installation in New England was a span over the Mill River in Hamden near Eli Whitney's gun factory; in 1980 an exact replica was built on what are probably the original piers.

In 1828 Town designed New Ha-

for their construction were ordered from Middletown and brought to New Haven by barge. New Haven's harbor was cut off by a squadron of British warships, but Commodore Hardy of the Royal Navy permitted the barges to pass through the blockade, saying that his fleet was not blockading religion. Hardy had commanded the H.M.S. *Victory* at Trafalgar and had held the dying Nelson in his arms.

Town was, however, best known for the design of the "Town bridge," a covered wooden bridge based struc-

ven's Third Congregational Church, which has long since disappeared if indeed it was ever built. Its design introduced a recessed porch fronted by two Doric columns *in antis,* an arrangement that became a favorite of the American Greek Revival.

In the early years of the 19th century, several newly rich New Haven citizens were able to build handsome homes and chose Town, or his partner Alexander Jackson Davis, as their architect. Davis designed the Classic Skinner home on Hillhouse Avenue in 1832, the Mary Pritchard house at 35 Hillhouse Avenue in 1836, and a home for a Mrs. Lent at 85 Trumbull Street the same year. Town designed and built his own Greek Revival home near the foot of Hillhouse Avenue. He was a scholar as well as a brilliant architect, and a handsome library on the second floor of his home contained his valuable collection of between nine and ten thousand books, most of them on architecture. Together, Town and Davis designed an elegant brick Greek Revival home for Ralph Ingersoll on Elm Street, facing the Green, and Davis crowned Hillhouse Avenue with a masterpiece, "Sachem's Wood," a stately Classic home for New Haven's leading citizen, James Hillhouse, atop the hill at the head of the avenue. In accordance with the will of a descendant, the house was dismantled in 1947. Its Classic interior details were restrained and delicate, and existing renderings of them by the architect are the delight of architectural historians. Town and Davis created the elegance of the Hillhouse Avenue area that was praised by Charles Dickens during his visit to America in 1842.

The magnificent elms that shaded so many of New Haven's streets for a century were planted at the instigation of James Hillhouse, who also was one of those instrumental in the founding of the new Burying Ground, the Grove Street Cemetery, surely a noteworthy architectural form.

In 1825 Town designed what would have been the handsome Greek Re-

vival Eagle Bank of New Haven, but the bank became insolvent just as construction was about to start. Renderings of the design that Town prepared for the bank are now in the library of the New Haven Colony Historical Society. His State Capitol (1827–1831) near the upper edge of the Green was the first Greek Doric temple in New England, and the vote of the citizens in 1887 to have it torn down was tragic. But Center Church remains as the masterpiece with which Ithiel Town's name is associated.

New Haven's early Colonial buildings were wood-frame and clapboard. Most of its distinguished Federal and Greek Revival buildings were of brick, but after the Civil War the exteriors of most of the city's new, important buildings were of either golden or rose-tinted chocolate-brown dressed stone, the golden rock quarried from East Rock or the Sleeping Giant, and the reddish chocolate brown from quarries in Fair Haven. A rose-tinted chocolate brown became New Haven's "own" color during the Brown Decades.

During the city's generally prosperous 19th century, there was a laying of the hands of the leading architect of one generation on his protégé of the next. Henry Austin (1804–1891), who had apprenticed under Town, became New Haven's leading and most prolific architect of the mid-19th century. Examples of his work have been found as far away as Maine and New Jersey. The Italianate style and towered villa were trademarks of his work. His New Haven railroad station, built in 1849, converted to a market in 1874 and destroyed by fire in 1894, was—aside from its exotic towers and trim—remarkably functional.

In 1842 Austin undertook the first of the number of interior remodelings that Center Church has undergone, and in 1845 the church exterior was painted a dreary olive-drab, only to regain the original richness of its red brick in 1912. During the 1890s, nine art-glass windows designed by Louis Comfort Tiffany's Glass and Decorat-

ing Company, and one attributed to John La Farge, replaced ten of the original windows of clear glass. Center Church was beautifully restored in 1960 by Carl Blanchard, a protégé of Douglas Orr. At that time nine of the art-glass windows were removed as the congregation felt, quite properly, that they were not compatible with the character of a Puritan meetinghouse. Three of them now decorate a wall in the Buley Library at Southern Connecticut State College and are handsomely mounted, framed, and backlighted. The others have also found appropriate homes. The one remaining Tiffany window in Center Church, designed by Joseph Lauber of Tiffany's staff, is located above the pulpit and depicts John Davenport preaching to the colonists on their first Sunday ashore in their new home.

The First Methodist Church at the

corner of College and Elm streets was one of Austin's designs. Originally it had a Tuscan flair, but it has undergone several changes of facade, the last being a new portico designed by Charles C. Haight of New York in 1904.

Austin designed scores of homes in and around New Haven, small and large. His practice spanned more than half a century and it has been said that there was an Austin-designed towered villa on virtually every street in the city. To Hillhouse Avenue he contributed number 24, the Dana house, and number 52, the Norton house. The Oliver B. North house at 604 Chapel Street is a Tuscan design that imparts a strong feeling of the Victorian age. The home he designed for Willis Bristol at 584 Chapel Street has ornate interior Italianate ornamental plaster that would be difficult to duplicate today, and several of its neighbors are known Austin designs or attributed to him.

Austin remodeled the Skinner home on Hillhouse Avenue, filling out its original cruciform plan, and added wings and a Tuscan tower to Ithiel Town's home which had been purchased by Joseph Sheffield. Elizabeth Mills Brown called the latter "a powerful presence"; to the dismay of architectural historians it was torn down in 1957 to make way for an inferior Yale laboratory.

In 1845 Austin designed the chocolate-brown landmark for which he is possibly best remembered, the massive gateway to the Grove Street Cemetery. His inspiration was derived, of course, from the temples and tombs of Egypt, and his choice of style was sound and appropriate.

In 1856 he designed the Tradesman's Bank on Orange Street, only recently razed. He is credited with the design of New Haven's High Victorian Gothic City Hall, with its soaring cast-iron staircase and rich oak paneling, a durable landmark of 1868 on Church Street facing the Green, but it was probably designed by his apprentice, protégé, and future partner David R. Brown. The design is durable, for its

facade has been incorporated into the new Civic Center designed by Herbert S. Newman in 1986.

The same year, Austin and Brown collaborated as partners on the design of the ebullient High Victorian Davies mansion at the crest of Prospect Hill. Its opulent interior made it the most splendid New Haven home of its day. Now belonging to Yale, it was about to fall victim to a wrecker's ball in 1980 but was saved at the last moment by the protests of concerned citizens, for which New Haveners and architectural historians everywhere will be forever thankful.

Sidney Mason Stone (1803–1882), a Connecticut carpenter who became a self-taught architect of considerable skill, was another prolific architect of the period. He designed and supervised the construction of many of the churches built in mid-19th century New Haven, and in a number of other cities as far away as Ohio—nearly a hundred in all. Although not of his design, St. Paul's Episcopal Church (1829) near Wooster Square is representative of his craftsmanship as a builder. He did design St. Michael's Roman Catholic Church, originally Wooster Square Congregational, but radical alterations have since been made and nearly every trace of his design and workmanship has been lost. In 1841 he designed the brownstone Third Congregational Church at the corner of Church and Court streets, opposite the Tontine Hotel. Third Congregational became the home of the New Haven Public Library. In 1849 he remodeled the interior of United Church on the Green, which was remodeled again and brought to its present-day pristine beauty by Gerald Watland in 1966. Stone designed the delicately proportioned, castle-like New Haven city jail on Whalley Avenue in 1857 which, despite the protests of the New Haven Preservation Trust and others, was razed in 1980.

This aptly named architect also designed a number of notable homes in

HENRY AUSTIN, ARCHITECT,
Office, Street's Building, Chapel St.
New Haven, Conn.

Top
Henry Austin remodeled the home of Ithiel Town on Hillhouse Avenue for Joseph Earl Sheffield, a railroad developer. A view of the house illustrated the capabilities of Austin's firm in this circa 1860 advertisement. (NHCHS)

Left
The building designed by Sidney Mason Stone for the Third Congregational Church can be seen across the Green in this 1909 photograph. At this juncture in its history it was the home of the New Haven Public Library. (NHCHS)

the city, including one for Ezekiel Trowbridge on Temple Street, which became a way-station of the underground railroad for escaping slaves and is now the Center Church parish house. His design for Thomas Trowbridge's home on Elm Street's "Quality Row" was a symbol of New Haven wealth and aristocracy and was greatly admired. The Peletiah Perit house at number 55 was his contribution to the grandeur of Hillhouse Avenue.

Stone was a man's man and was at one time captain of the New Haven Grays, the city's elite membership-by-invitation-only military company. At the outbreak of the Civil War he was offered command of a volunteer regiment but declined because of his age.

During the latter part of the 19th century, New Haven's maritime importance dwindled and its prosperity

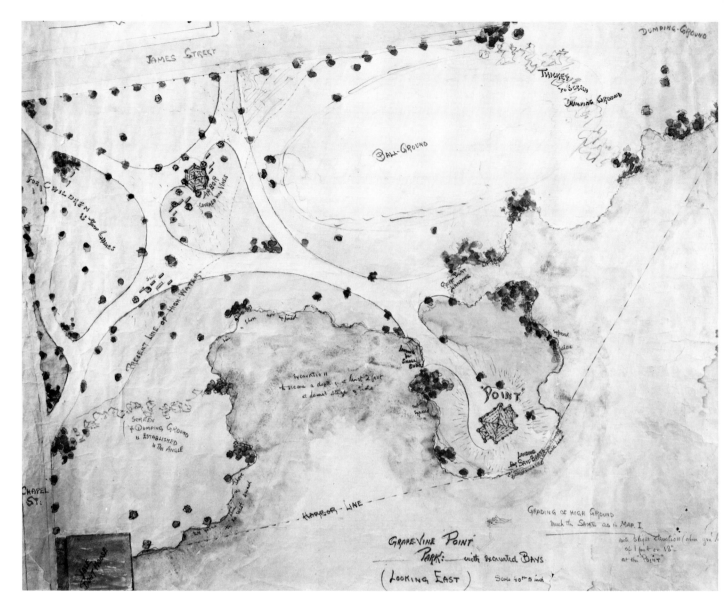

Donald Grant Mitchell's careful attention to landscape design is evident in his proposal for Grapevine Point Park. (NHCHS)

became based instead on its strength as a manufacturing center. Eli Whitney's gun factory at the edge of the city was absorbed by mighty Winchester Arms, producer of repeating rifles that "won the West." Candee Rubber was the largest manufacturer of rubber boots and shoes in the world, and the New Haven Clock Company the largest manufacturer of mass-produced timepieces in the United States. Sargent was a major manufacturer of hardware, as it is today, and the goods and passengers to and from all New England were moved over the tracks of the New Haven Railroad, as they are

not today. Yale was spreading out and flexing its muscles as a great world university. It was indeed a golden age for New Haven. Fortunes were made; middle-managers and craftsmen lived well. This was reflected in the city's fine civic and commercial buildings and in its elegant homes.

The prestigious homes of Quality Row facing the north side of the Green were owned by Sargents (hardware) and Trowbridges (West Indies trade), and those of Hillhouse Avenue by Farnams, Townsends, Sheffields, and more Trowbridges. Handsome but less pretentious homes ringed Wooster Square and reached out along Whitney Avenue toward Hamden, and out Chapel Street toward Westville. They were of varied sizes and built of various materials. Often the exteriors were of native dressed brownstone, and together they made a cosmopolitan whole, reflecting a vigor and prosperity that provided ample outlet for the talents of busy New Haven architects.

Most of the city's late 19th-century architects trained under Henry Austin. David R. Brown (1831–1910) was his special protégé and briefly his partner. In 1868, as a designer in Austin's employ, he worked on the design of City Hall, and with Austin designed the quite overpowering Davies mansion. Brown designed the massive Trinity Lutheran Church, originally the Congregational Church of the Redeemer, and collaborated with Donald Grant Mitchell in the design of the Connecticut Building at the Centennial Exposition in Philadelphia in 1876, a very Victorian interpretation of a Colonial Connecticut home.

Donald Grant Mitchell (1822–1908), a writer, horticulturist, and talented amateur architect, deserves mention. A "man for all seasons," his proposals were in the form of delicate watercolor renderings for East Rock and other city public parks. Several of these, now in the library of the New Haven Colony Historical Society, were followed almost to the last pathway when they were built in the early 1880s. His baronial home in Westville attracted New Haven's intellectual elite, and Mitchell was a prolific writer under both his own name and the pseudonym "Ik Marvel."

Late in the 19th century, David Brown formed a partnership with German-born Ferdinand von Beren. Their firm dominated the New Haven turn-of-the-century architectural scene, designing city schools, public buildings, and scores of homes, many of which are still standing today, including the Grave mansion on a prominent slope in Hamden, which now houses the offices of Roche-Dinkeloo and Associates, an architectural firm of national renown.

Rufus Russell (1823–1896) was another Austin apprentice who later had a busy architectural practice of his own. He designed the old police building on Court Street, several city schools, and dozens of robust High Victorian homes. In 1871 he designed the Calvary Baptist Church which today, minus its steeple and with an entirely new interior, is the Yale Repertory Theatre. The following year he designed the Davenport Congregational Church, now St. Casimir's Roman Catholic, another church in the Wooster Square area. Several hundred delightful renderings done by Russell and his draftsmen are in the architectural drawings collection of the New Haven Colony Historical Society.

In New Haven during the first decades of the 20th century, as in the rest of New England, there was an architectural return to the Federal and neo-Colonial styles. J. Frederick Kelly's (1888–1947) handsome homes, restorations, and the headquarters of the New Haven Colony Historical Society are fine, well-proportioned, and carefully detailed designs typical of these years. Roughly contemporary with Kelly's work was that of Leoni W. Robinson (d. 1923), another Austin apprentice, many of whose designs, such as the First Baptist Church (1903) at the corner of Edwards and Livingston streets, drew their inspiration from the Richardson Romanesque. Robinson made complete measured drawings of Center Church in 1912, a monumental undertaking.

The mid-20th century belonged to Douglas Orr (1892–1966); his opulent "Town and Country" neo-Colonial designs, best represented by the elegant New Haven Lawn Club and the Quinnipiac Club, are handsome indeed. In 1938 Orr collaborated with R. W. Foote, an older architect and friend, in the design of the almost pure Art Deco headquarters office building of the Southern New England Telephone Company. Foote made major contributions to the design, and no hand-

somer office building has ever been built in New Haven.

Orr was less at home in the contemporary style. His arresting First Church of Christ Scientist (1950) on Whitney Avenue is eye-catching but rigid; the headquarters office building of the New York, New Haven and Hartford Railroad (1946) and the headquarters of the 1st New Haven Bank (1960) are merely typical of their time. But the Georgian Church of the Redeemer, in large measure the creation of his associate "Ding" Palmer, is handsome and beautifully proportioned. His contemporary design for Connecticut Blue Shield, also on Whitney Avenue, is concise and timeless. Although overshadowed by major projects, a stream of designs of attractive comfortable homes flowed from the drafting boards of Orr's office, usually executed in his stylish neo-Colonial manner. His residential work ranged from large public housing projects to mansions. A dozen Douglas Orr buildings line Church Street and Whitney Avenue, and there are dozens more throughout the city. Orr designed more projects, many of them remodelings, for Yale than any other architect in its history, and he left an indelible stamp on the city. He had an engaging personality and special qualities of personal leadership. He served as president of the American Institute of Architects between 1947 and 1949, and as a director of several New Haven charitable, civic, and social organizations; he was a great, public-spirited citizen.

Certain New Haven buildings stand out because of their historical or architectural interest, or simply because their location makes them landmarks. The Pardee-Morris house near Morris Cove on the eastern shore of the harbor is a survivor of the 18th century, and

a few of its thick masonry walls date from about 1680; it was added to about 1767. During the night of July 5, 1779, it was burned by British troops shortly after their amphibious landing on the shore of Morris Cove, but the walls, chimneys, and some timbers survived and the Morris House was rebuilt. Its plan is rambling and there is a small ballroom on the second floor. Today it is preserved by the New Haven Colony Historical Society and between May and October is open to the public at certain hours without charge.

Closer in is "Raynham," originally a spacious Federal home built in 1804 on a baronial suburban estate, converted to Carpenter Gothic in 1856. It is a colorful piece of Gothic Revival fancy, impeccably maintained by descendants of its original owners.

The corner of Church and Chapel streets is the traditional hub of downtown New Haven, and since 1832 The Exchange, a four-story Greek Revival commercial building has occupied the northeast corner. Extant photographs show soldiers lined up beside it as they left for the Civil War, and even then it was a generation old. Today it is poorly maintained and its street level has been garishly remodeled to accommodate a series of cut-rate drug stores, but the fenestration above is calm and orderly. Elizabeth Mills Brown suggests that the design might be Ithiel Town's; the builder is known to have been Atwater Treat. For years the building was owned by Yale as a rental income investment, but new owners have hinted at its demolition and replacement by a contemporary high-rise structure.

James Gamble Rogers' design for the Post Office and Federal Building on Church Street provided a suitably grand setting for the United States government. Construction barriers provided a handy place to advertise bonds during World War I. Photo by T. S. Bronson. (NHCHS)

Facing page
The Soldiers and Sailors Monument at the summit of East Rock was photographed by Myron W. Filley shortly after it was dedicated in 1887. (NHCHS)

The city's days of industrial might are reflected in the McLagon Foundry of 1870 at the lower end of Whitney Avenue, tastefully restored and converted to shops, offices, and an attractive restaurant a century later by Charles Brewer; the restaurant wing in the rear was remodeled by John Fowler. Like other late 19th-century New Haven factories, it is of unadorned red brick, but the texture of the brick imparts a feeling of rugged strength and interest. The McLagon Foundry is architectural restoration at its best.

Apart from the city, yet very much a part of it, the Soldiers and Sailors Monument rises to a height of 110 feet above the top of East Rock. Designed by Moffatt and Doyle of New York, it was built at the instigation of the Admiral Foote Post of the G.A.R. Civil War veterans, and was dedicated with fireworks and civic festivities on June 17, 1887. Myriad bas-reliefs and sculptures on and around an ornate shaft which stands on a rectangular base depict important events in American military history; the names of New Haven men who fell in American wars between the Revolutionary and the Civil wars are inscribed on its base. The dra-

matic view of the city from the park that surrounds it has attracted picnickers, hikers, sightseers and, on moonlit nights, lovers, for a century.

Christ Church Episcopal on Broadway has never received the praise it deserves. A seat of the high Anglican ritual, it was designed in 1895 by Henry Vaughan, an accomplished, British-trained church architect of the day from Boston. Its exterior of reddish Fair Haven brownstone is not exceptional, but its soaring brick interior, carved rood screen, baptismal font, stone reredos, and exciting Victorian art-glass windows brought from England go far beyond both Gothic Revival and High Victorian and approach the pure Gothic, providing a rich background for the ritual of its services.

In 1913 the venerable Tontine Hotel built by David Hoadley gave way to the first of James Gamble Rogers's many New Haven buildings, the Classic post office and federal district court at the corner of Church and Court streets. Its monumentality changed the scale of the block, but its character is properly representative of our national government.

Across Court Street, on the former

site of Sidney Mason Stone's Third Congregational Church, R. W. Foote's Powell Building (1921) stood for sixty-five years. It was a handsome twelve-story building, but each floor was small and the structure was never economic. It was demolished in 1986 to make way for a new high-rise building that will be a part of the rebuilt City Hall and Civic Center complex.

Buildings on the southeast corner of College and Chapel streets have provided a home away from home for visitors to New Haven for more than two

centuries. The first was the Beers Tavern where George Washington once slept. It was replaced in 1851 by the New Haven House, a Henry Austin design, which was the scene of countless banquets and the overnight abode of Yale parents and prom dates for 60 years. In 1911 it was replaced in turn by the Hotel Taft, the city's elegant hotel for the next half century. The Taft was dignified but devoid of local character. Its demise as a hotel coincided with New Haven's decline as an industrial center. After being vacant for a decade it has been converted into

apartments, and there are surely many more years of usefulness ahead for it in its new role.

Over the years the growth of a city leads to the replacement of many fine buildings by newer structures more appropriate to the changing times, and New Haven is no exception. Most of Quality Row, the patrician homes on Elm Street facing the New Haven Green, are gone, but two of the buildings that replace them are handsome and appropriate—the public library, designed by Cass Gilbert in 1908, and the New Haven County Courthouse by William H. Allen and Richard Williams the following year. Yale's Hendrie Hall (1894), a Venetian palazzo designed by Cady Berg and See, popular New York architects of the time, is less appropriate and out of scale. "Sachem's Wood" at the head of Hillhouse Avenue was dismantled in accordance with a will, and the striking group of buildings that replaces it will be distinguished in any age. Inevitably, numbers of other architecturally valuable homes have also disappeared.

But some losses could have been avoided and will always be felt. In 1957 Yale demolished the Ithiel Town home that had been remodeled and enlarged by Henry Austin, and erected an undistinguished laboratory in its place. In 1889 Ithiel Town's beautiful State Capitol on the Green was razed, an irreplaceable loss.

The pros and cons of Yale's replacement of the Old Brick Row, its Colonial campus for more than a century, will always be debated. Undoubtedly the aging brick buildings had become structurally unsound and unsanitary, and individually they were not the handsomest of Colonial buildings. Their charm was in their presence as a related group, the first planned college campus in America.

From the 1830s until the end of the century, the elegance of York Square rivaled that of Hillhouse Avenue and Quality Row. The handsome homes that surrounded the private elm-shaded park were in turn enclosed by a common iron fence; the whole enclave could be closed off by an iron gate. The park was owned by the families living around it and York Square was a private subcommunity of great charm. The east side of the square fell victim to a new city high school and a trade school in 1901, the north side to another school a few years later. Then Grove Street in the form of Tower Parkway was extended through the heart of the park. Finally, in 1930, two handsome Greek Revival homes on the west side of the square were razed to make way for the Payne Whitney Gymnasium, and the grace of York Square became only a memory.

During the first half of the 19th century, New Haven's port was a busy one—the city traded with the world. Today there is no trace of the buildings that housed its ship chandlers and countinghouses, and indeed no physical trace of this phase of New Haven history remains at all. The city is now separated from its harbor by one superhighway and cut in half by another. New Haven can never re-create the flavor of its early 19th-century harbor and wharves as has, for example, Boston.

The deterioration of the dignity of its streets is, however, New Haven's greatest architectural and environmental loss. Like The Exchange at the corner of Church and Chapel streets, scores of handsome, well-proportioned, early and mid-19th-century buildings have been defaced by the tasteless conversion of their ground floors into fast-food emporia and unattractive discount stores. Should one glance above these ground floors, one often sees fine moldings and delicate Federal details. Thoughtful urban renewal would preserve and restore this architectural heritage for the city, and well-conceived attempts are being made in this direction today by both private owners and public agencies.

Legislation in the late 1940s created new concepts of federal funding for urban renewal, and New Haven's Mayor Richard Lee, an executive of great energy, ability, vision, and integrity, aggressively and successfully sought federal funds with which to virtually rebuild the central part of the city. He staffed the Redevelopment Agency with the best available talent, and nationally known architects drew plans for New Haven's urban renewal projects, many of which replaced blocks of miserable slums. The city's dramatic urban renewal efforts drew worldwide attention; it was an exhilarating time for New Haven.

These were the early days of planned urban renewal when cities received shock therapy that often did not lead to the realization of original hopes. In retrospect it is apparent that the city's vast urban renewal program of the 1950s and early 1960s did not re-create the vigorous downtown urban core that was expected of it, despite the talents and funds expended. Substantial numbers of older office buildings, stores, small shops, and homes were razed. Blocks of residential slums were leveled, unfortunately without earnest consideration of any intrinsic period-piece architectural character and pos-

The demolition of Ithiel Town's State Capitol behind Center Church on the Green was carried out over the protests of many New Haven citizens. These remarkable photographs document the fall of the six columns of the north portico. Seven men turned the windlass connected to the iron cables that passed through holes cut above the east and west columns. The columns began to crack under the pressure and finally fell forward to the cheers of 3,000 onlookers. (NHCHS)

The rare treasures contained in Yale University's Beinecke Library are sumptuously housed inside the translucent marble walls of Gordon Bunshaft's design. Courtesy, Yale University.

sibilities for restoration that parts of them might have had. The stub of a superhighway which might have curved around the city and which, twenty-seven years later, has not yet been completed was led into its heart, a wound that may never be healed.

In return, New Haven received apartment towers, commercial structures, a new downtown hotel, and an enclosed shopping mall that, while sleek and modern, are not architecturally noteworthy. The mall is served by Paul Rudolph's stunning sculptural parking garage in which it is difficult to park one's car. Construction-cost overruns caused drastic cutbacks in the construction of Roche-Dinkeloo and Associates' Coliseum, diluting its usefulness and spoiling its exterior elevations. Richard Lee's visions of a rejuvenated urban core that would attract shoppers and commercial enterprise have not yet been realized; may the 21st century see them come true!

Unquestionably, the areas that were bulldozed needed renewal badly. Most of them had deteriorated into outright slums. But some of the buildings within them undoubtedly were basically sound and of period-piece architectural value worthy of preservation. None was spared. Had New Haven's dynamic

urban renewal program been carried out a quarter of a century later it surely would have been implemented with far greater sensitivity, and the result would have preserved the unity, architectural tradition, and character of the city to a far greater degree.

The 1960s brought the Knights of Columbus and Coliseum complex to lower Church Street on land that urban renewal had cleared. Designed by Roche-Dinkeloo and Associates, the Knights of Columbus building has at each corner a strong but curious masonry tower of a rich New Haven brown with a purple cast, intended to complement even stronger round elements of the Coliseum. But the intended effect was spoiled because the round elements of the Coliseum fell victim to the construction-cost overruns and were never built. By virtue of its height alone, the Knights of Columbus Tower has become a city landmark.

In recent years New Haven and Yale have become showcases of fine contemporary design. Herbert S. Newman and Associates' design for the new City Hall will adjoin the durable High Victorian Gothic facade of Henry Austin's city hall in a way that will respect the dignity of the old building and harmonize with it. William

Pedersen's Federal Building and New Haven Savings Bank stand behind and beside City Hall, and a swirling, colorful contemporary sculpture, *On High* (1980), by Alexander Lieberman of New York, completes the new Civic Center. Together they set the stage for New Haven in the 21st century.

The exterior of Herbert S. Newman and Associates' racy Teletrack complex expresses a feeling of the activity within. Marcel Breuer (of Bauhaus fame) and Robert F. Gatji's Armstrong Rubber headquarters of precast concrete units create a strong gateway to the city as one drives by the contemporary structures in the city's partially successful close-in industrial park that faces the Connecticut Turnpike, and the exciting new Fusco post-modern office building development along the south shore of the harbor holds promise of a revitalized future for New Haven's close-in shoreline.

Yale's buildings are an integral part of the story of New Haven architecture and are a fascinating cornucopia of architectural styles. Beginning in 1800 with Peter Banner and his North Middle College and Connecticut Lyceum, Yale has consistently commissioned distinguished architects to design its buildings, and generally its buildings have reflected the best of the architectural styles of their day. The Yale campus is a cavalcade of the history of American architecture; Yale's physical character is both subtle and powerful. It has been proposed that the special loyalty of Yale alumni to their alma mater is generated by the beauty of its buildings and the environment they create. The campus can be described in terms of its color, texture, and magnificent architectural vistas.

Tradition has it that the exterior of the first Yale building in New Haven was daubed with a mixture of lampblack, whited lead, and oil, but beginning with Connecticut Hall in 1750, the Old Brick Row made Yale a rich red, relieved by white trim, Colonial cupolas, and, after 1832, the white of the art gallery John Trumbull designed to house the paintings he had given to the college. As the High Victorian Old Campus evolved during the latter part of the 19th century, Yale became a rose-tinted New Haven brown of stone and brick, pleasantly compatible with the green of spring and summer, a glorious combination with the fall foliage, but stark and forbidding during the gloom of winter. In 1901 the enclave of off-white Classic bicentennial buildings, designed in the spirit of the Columbian Exposition of 1893, brought a welcome contrast to Yale's chocolate-brown decades.

Beginning with James Gamble Rogers's Harkness Memorial Quadrangle in 1917, Yale's magnificent second-generation neo-Gothic courtyards of the 1920s and 1930s were of a warmer more sophisticated golden beige and light gray stone, which also mellowed the New Haven brown, and these in turn were relieved by the rich red of the tower of the Hall of Graduate Studies (1932) and the Law School (1931). All of these neo-Gothic buildings were highly acclaimed when they were built, but the next generation denigrated them for what it considered their slavish imitation or, at best, slick adaptation of true Gothic. Today, however, they once again receive the admiration they deserve, for their materials, carved woodwork and stone, and the delicate tracery of their fenestration will not be matched in our time, or that of our children's children.

In the late 1930s and 1940s, the red of the newer Georgian residential colleges balanced the tones of the Collegiate Gothic. After World War II, Yale's vast construction program brought a potpourri of color to the campus: the warm beige of Eero Saarinen's residential colleges (1961); the reddish-purple and brown of Philip Johnson's science buildings (1964); the stark whites of Marcel Breuer's Engineering and Applied Science building (1968); and Skidmore, Owings and Merrill's Beinecke Rare Book and Manuscript Library (1963), a jewel case for Yale's greatest literary treasures, designed by Gordon

Henry Austin's monumental design for the entrance to Grove Street Cemetery appears as immovable as the fact of death itself.

Facing page
The courtyards of Yale's residential colleges offer an escape from the rigors of academia. Branford College Court and Wrexham Tower are much the same today as when they were photographed by T. S. Bronson in the 1920s. (NHCHS)

Bunshaft. Its mixture of strong colors has always brought a sense of excitement to the campus.

Yale's architectural vistas are rich and exciting, too. A noted city planner has called the visual impact of a walk through Phelps Gateway and under Phelps Tower (Charles C. Haight, 1896) one of the strongest in all American architecture. First, Henry Austin's splendid Gothic Revival library (1842), remodeled as a chapel in 1930 by Day and Klauder of Philadelphia, prominent college architects of the day, is silhouetted in the arch of the gateway, but just off-center, which invites interest. In a moment, James Gamble Rogers's graceful Gothic Harkness Memorial Tower (1917), today the symbol of Yale, comes into view. Rogers's chief designer, the eccentric Otto Faelton, based the design scheme on the Butter Tower in Rouen; later Faelton became a beloved teacher of architecture at Yale. Finally, as one emerges from beneath Phelps Tower, the calm dignity of the Old Campus unfolds itself impressively.

The view from the plaza steps of the Carrère and Hastings Memorial Hall rotunda (1901) tells the story of the progression of 20th-century American architecture. The Classic Commons with its stately Corinthian colonnade (1901 and 1927) is to the right; to the left are Classic Woolsey Hall and French Renaissance Woodbridge Hall (both 1901). In the foreground, across the Hewitt University Quadrangle plaza, is the unique Beinecke Library with its sunken courtyard and symbolic sculp-

ture by Isamu Noguchi. Behind it are arrayed the beige-gray Collegiate Gothic of Berkeley College (1934), the soaring neo-Gothic tower of the Sterling Memorial Library (1927–1930), and the delicate tracery of the windows of the Sterling Law School library, inspired by King's College, Cambridge, but certainly not a copy. The latter three are the creations of James Gamble Rogers and his stable of skilled Gothic designers and draftsmen. The tracery of the Law School library windows was designed and detailed, curve by curve, by Wesley Needham, a self-taught Gothic draftsman who later taught himself the Tibetan language and became curator of Yale's collection of rare Tibetan manuscripts. The vista is introduced by a dignified flagpole and a vibrant, colorful Calder mobile. As a complete whole, this architectural vista is breathtaking. The tower of the Hall of Graduate Studies terminates the upward slope of Wall Street, creating another effective vista nearby.

Even without the elms, Hillhouse Avenue is impressive. Philip Johnson's strong and colorful Kline Biology Tower has replaced "Sachem's Wood" as its focal point. The tower was sited just to the left of the avenue's centerline, and the Gibbs Laboratory of Physics (Douglas Orr with Paul Schweikher, 1955) just to the right, a carefully studied balance that is visually rewarding. On the avenue, at number 43 on the right, is the home of Yale presidents, originally a Victorian fortress designed by Russell Sturgis in 1871 for Henry Far-

nam, New Haven railroad financier. It became handsomely Georgian in 1934, remodeled by Kimball and Husted, but lost much of its original vigor in the transition. On the left, Alexander Jackson Davis's Apthorp home and Henry Austin's Tuscan-towered Norton home next door were sensitively integrated into Yale's School of Organization and Management complex by Edward Larrabee Barnes in 1978.

The carefully studied promenade between Eero Saarinen's Morse and Stiles colleges created another stunning vista that changes with every step. As one proceeds, the Gothic tower of the Payne Whitney Gymnasium (1934), John Russell Pope's *aedes sudoris*, is gradually unveiled, finally standing majestically alone.

The Kline Biology Tower crowns yet another but generally unappreciated vista. Looking north from the head of Broadway, up Tower Parkway, the silhouette of the distant tower is bracketed by the gold and gray of the gymnasium and the beige stone and concrete towers of Stiles College, inspired by the villages of northern Italy. The mile-long vista enables one to grasp the full scope of Yale's architectural depth.

The Sterling Memorial Library viewed from College Street is the terminus of a majestic vista, and again as it is viewed from the tiny, charming "Potty" courtyard of Trumbull College. And it is important to the walk from Noah Porter Gateway (Howells and Stokes, 1912) to the bright (too bright on a sunny day) Hewitt University Quadrangle and the Memorial Colonnade beyond.

Although examples of neo-Classic and Federal Revival designs are wanting, the parade of buildings up Chapel Street that are devoted to the study, display, and practice of art at Yale otherwise depicts the flow of American architectural design since the Civil War. Peter B. Wight's High Victorian Gothic Street Hall (1864), the first college art-school building in America, leads off the parade, and Egerton Swartwout's Tuscan Romanesque bridge over High Street joins it to his old Art Gallery (both 1928) with its exquisite Samuel Yellin iron grillwork. These expand into Louis Kahn's (with Douglas Orr and Associates) new Art Gallery (1953), a stunning contemporary design that time may prove to be the most timeless of all Yale buildings. In 1978 Herbert S. Newman skillfully buried a handsome lecture hall under it. Then across York Street, Paul Rudolph's Brutal Contemporary Art and Architecture building winds up the parade. Of the latter, Elizabeth Mills Brown says, "What no one disputes is its magnificent presence," certainly a magnificent understatement. Across Chapel Street is the opulent, sleek, steel-clad Yale Center for British Art (1968–1977), the brilliant Louis Kahn's last work.

At the other end of the Yale campus, just beyond the crest of Prospect Hill, Delano and Aldrich created the vista that is the Yale Divinity School (1929–1931). An interpretation of Thomas Jefferson's "Lawn" at the University of Virginia, the complex is beautifully sited and graded on slowly rising land; the Jeffersonian colonnade culminates in a Federal Revival chapel whose puritan interior is somewhat marred by incongruous Art Deco chandeliers. The integrated whole is a reflection of the prosperous late 1920s, and the interconnected buildings are delicately scaled, suave Federal Revival design at its best.

In no other American city are such fine examples of every style and period of American architecture so plentiful and accessible as in New Haven. From the early Colonial to the Brutal phase of the Contemporary, the city is dotted with homes and civic, commercial, and university buildings of extraordinary quality that are collectively representative of the entire spectrum of American architectural design. New Haven has them all, virtually side by side. In this sense, New Haven is a handsomely filled showcase of American history.

COLOR PLATES

Samual F. B. Morse painted inventor-entrepreneur Eli Whitney circa 1822. (NHCHS)

When L. Schierholz painted this view of New Haven from Fair Haven Heights circa 1860, the industries that would make New Haven famous were only wisps of smoke on the horizon. From the collection of Ellen B. Sherk.

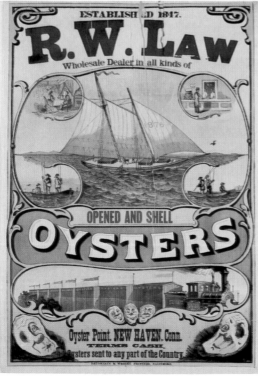

Top
*William Giles Munson's View
of New Haven Green in 1800
shows the 1763 statehouse, the
brick meetinghouse of the First
Society, and the wood meetinghouse of the Fair Haven Society.*
(NHCHS)

Left
*Succulent oysters from the waters
of New Haven Harbor and Long
Island Sound were shipped to all
parts of the United States by com-
panies such as R. W. Law at
Oyster Point in the last century.*
(NHCHS)

Left
Cinqué, the Mendi warrior and leader of the Amistad captives, was painted by Nathaniel Jocelyn in 1839. (NHCHS)

Below
The Morris family rebuilt its home in Morris Cove after it was burned by the British in 1779. The large kitchen in the western ell of the building (below left) and the southwest parlor (below) are two of the many period rooms open to the public during the summer months. (NHCHS)

The roof of the New Haven House Hotel provided a sweeping vista of the three churches and Greek Revival statehouse on New Haven Green for artist Thomas P. Rossiter in the mid-19th century. (NHCHS)

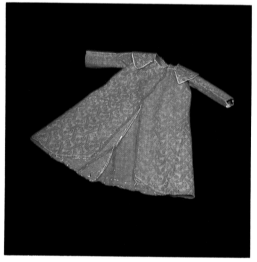

Above
This bright red wool coat worn by Simon Tuttle, born in New Haven in 1647, belies the notion that Puritan colonists were unfailingly grim and somber. (NHCHS)

Above right
New Haven's silver industry is represented by this William North and Company tea service fashioned about 1815. (NHCHS)

New Haven's direct trade with Europe was carried out in ships like the Sparking Sea, *shown leaving Messina, Italy, in 1860 by William Bygrave. (NHCHS)*

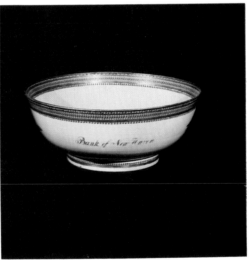

Above
The view of New Haven Green on J. and J. Jackson's Staffordshire vegetable dish was based on an 1831 engraving by A. J. Davis. (NHCHS)

Above right
This Chinese export punch bowl was presented to the Bank of New Haven during the height of the China Trade period. (NHCHS)

Above
A weathered dock on the Quinnipiac River points to the Front Street section of Fair Haven, a unique residential area in the midst of the city. Fair Haven's 18th- and 19th-century houses are being restored through the dedicated efforts of private individuals.

Right
A view of Yale taken through Phelps Gateway on the Old Campus.

Autumn foliage frames the Bennett Memorial Drinking Fountain and the office tower of the Chapel Square Mall.

Facing page
The Graduate and Faculty clubs at Yale University offer 20th-century hospitality in the 18th-century settings of the Jonathan Mix and John Pierpont houses on the Green.

Right
A Federal barn at the Eli Whitney Armory site houses performances and exhibits sponsored by the Eli Whitney Museum.

Below
The New Haven Colony Historical Society is headquartered in this handsome Whitney Avenue structure designed by architect J. Frederick Kelly, who worked in New Haven during the first half of the 20th century. (NHCHS)

The three churches on the Green: Trinity Episcopal, Center, and United. Ithiel Town's designs for Trinity Episcopal Church and Center Church reflect the different heritage of the two congregations, while David Hoadley's design for United Church affirms the historical bonds it shares with Center Church.

The buildings on the Yale University campus offer a fascinating array of colors and architectural styles. In the late 1930s and 1940s the rich red color of the Georgian residential colleges, such as this one, balanced the tones of the Collegiate Gothic.

165

This overview of the city of New Haven shows the variety of architectural styles that can still be found today.

Above right
A pretty, white wooden portico draws attention to this red-brick house located on Wooster Square.

Right
Partially framed in foliage, this view of the city was taken from East Rock.

REFERENCES AND NOTES

Chapter I References

Atwater, Edward E., *History of the Colony of New Haven*, Meriden, Journal Publishing Company, 1902. Useful only for the documents it contains.

Bailyn, Bernard, *The New England Merchants in the Seventeenth Century*, Cambridge, Harvard University Press, 1955. A scholarly work that contains a great deal of information about New Haven.

Black, Robert C., *The Younger John Winthrop*. New York, Columbia University Press, 1966. An outstanding biography of a man important to both Connecticut and New Haven.

Brown, Elizabeth Mills, manuscript of a paper on the designer of New Haven, to be published in the *Journal* of the new Haven Colony Historical Society. A fine example of historical detective work.

Calder, Isabel MacBeath, *The New Haven Colony*, New Haven, Yale University Press, 1934. A dull but informative volume.

Dexter, Franklin Bowditch, ed., *Ancient Town Records; New Haven Town Records, 1649–1662*, New Haven, New Haven Colony Historical Society, 1917.

_____, ed., *Ancient Town Records; New Haven Town Records, 1662–1684*, New Haven, New Haven Colony Historical Society, 1919. These two volumes, together with the succeeding Powers volume, are the single most useful source on early New Haven.

Farnham, Thomas Jr., and Sheldon J. Watts, *New Haven: The Earliest Years*, New Haven, New Haven Bicentennial Commission, 1976.

Farnham, Thomas J., and Sheldon J. Watts, *New Haven: 1660–1763*, New Haven, New Haven Bicentennial Commission, 1976. Two brief volumes that consist of accurate but disjointed vignettes of early New Haven.

Osterweis, Rollin G., *The New Haven Green and the American Revolution*, Hamden, Archon Books, 1976. An interesting story of an interesting landmark.

_____, *Three Centuries of New Haven: The Tercentenary History*, New Haven, Yale University Press, 1953. A solid, interestingly written history. The logical place to begin any study of the city's past.

Powers, Zara Jones, *Ancient Town Records; New Haven Town Records, 1684–1769*, New Haven, New Haven Colony Historical Society, 1962.

Shumway, Floyd M., Early New Haven and Its Leadership, Ph.D. dissertation, Columbia University, 1968. The best study of early New Haven available, part of which has been published in the *Journal* of the New Haven Colony Historical Society, September, 1972, vol. XXI, pp. 45-67.

Taylor, Robert J., *Colonial Connecticut*, Millwood, New York, KTO Press, 1979. A modern survey of the colony's development.

Chapter I Notes

[1] Calder, *The New Haven Colony*, p. 4.

[2] Osterweis, *Three Centuries*, p. 8.

[3] *Ibid*.

[4] Calder, *The New Haven Colony*, p.53.

[5] Brown, manuscript.

[6] Atwater, *History of the Colony of New Haven*, Appendix I.

[7] Shumway, p. 61; Farnham and Watts, *The Earliest Years*, p. 26.

[8] Farnham and Watts, *The Earliest Years*, p. 16.

[9] Osterweis, *Three Centuries*, p. 32.

[10] Bailyn, *The New England Merchant in the Seventeenth Century*, p. 95.

[11] Farnham and Watts, *The Earliest Years*, p. 33.

[12] Black, *The Younger John Winthrop*, p. 176.

[13] Farnham and Watts, *1660–1763*, pp. 34-35.

[14] Calder, *The New Haven Colony*, pp. 258-259.

Chapter II Notes

[1] The May 1726 session of the General Assembly requested the towns to work out plans for "the utter destroying" of barberry bushes because it was believed that they caused blast or rust in wheat. *Ancient Town Record, III, New Haven Town Records*, ed. Zara Jones Powers, New Haven, New Haven Colony Historical Society, 1962, pp. 409n, 567n.

[2] Richard D. Brown, *Modernization, the Transformation of American Life*, New York, Hill and Wang, 1976, pp. 12–15.

[3] Rollin G. Osterweis, *Three Centuries of New Haven, 1638–1938*, New Haven, Yale University Press, 1953; Edward E. Atwater, ed., *History of the City of New Haven to the Present Time*, New York, W. W. Munsell & Co., 1887; and J. L. Rockey, ed., *History of New Haven County, Connecticut*, vol. I, New York, W. W. Preston & Co., 1892; and the *Town Records*, vol. III, are the sources of all the historical descriptions and quotations in this chapter, unless otherwise noted.

[4] Richard L. Bushman, *From Puritan to Yankee, Character and the Social Order*, Cambridge, Harvard University Press, 1967, pp. 207, 211, and passim.

[5] Leonard Bacon, *Thirteen Historical Discourses on the Completion of Two Hundred Years, from the Beginning of the First Church in New Haven*, New Haven, Durrie & Peck, 1839, pp. 198–210. A basic study of the Great Awakening is by Edwin Scott Gausted, *The Great Awakening in New England*, Gloucester, Mass., Peter Smith, 1965. An interesting documentary history is provided by Stephen Nissenbaum, *The Great Awakening at Yale College*, Belmont, Calif., Wadsworth Publishing Company, Inc., 1972.

[6] Thomas J. Farnham, Mary Davis Farnham, and Sheldon J. Watts, *New Haven: The Making of a Modern Community*, vol. III, *The Bicentennial Radio Series*, New Haven, The New Haven Bicentennial Commission, 1976. Also see Carolyn Cooper, Merrill Lindsay, et al., *Eli Whitney and the Whitney Armory*, Whitneyville, Conn., Eli Whitney Museum, 1980.

[7] Charles Roy Keller, *The Second Great Awakening in Connecticut*, New Haven, Yale University Press, 1942, p. 3.

[8] Richard D. Brown, *Modernization, the Transformation of American Life*, p. 186.

Chapter III References

Dahl, Robert, *Who Governs? Democracy and Power in an American City,* New Haven, Yale University Press, 1961.

Warner, Robert, *New Haven Negroes,* New Haven, Yale University Press, 1940.

Wolfinger, Raymond, *The Politics of Progress,* Englewood Cliffs, Prentice-Hall, 1974.

Chapter IV Notes

[1] Richard Pares, *Yankees and Creoles: The Trade between North America and the West Indies before the Revolution* (Cambridge, Mass., 1956); Franklin B. Dexter, 'The New Haven of Two Hundred Years Ago,"*Papers of the New Haven Colony Historical Society,* VIII (New Haven, 1914), 329–50.

[2] The occupations of householders in the inner town are graphically noted in the Wadsworth map of 1748 reproduced in Rollin G. Osterweis, *Three Centuries of New Haven* (New Haven, 1953).

[3] *Connecticut Journal,* Jan. 12, Feb. 16, Nov. 9, 1780; May 15, 1783; July 7, Aug. 11, Dec. 8, 1784.

[4] Thomas R. Trowbridge, Jr., *History of the Ancient Maritime Interests of New Haven* (New Haven, 1882), chapter VII.

Chapter V Notes

[1] Fuller, Grace P., *An Introduction to the History of Connecticut as a Manufacturing State,* Smith College Studies in History, October 1915, p. 27.

[2] Dwight, Timothy, *A Statistical Account of the City of New Haven,* Connecticut Academy of Arts and Sciences, vol. 1, no. 1, 1811.

[3] *Benham's New Haven Directory,* 1872–1873.

[4] Chandler, George B., "Industrial History," in Osborn, Norris Galpin, ed., *History of Connecticut,* New York: States History Co., 1925, vol. 4, p. 31.

Chapter VI References

Atwater, Edward E., ed., *History of the Colony of New Haven to the Present Time,* New York, W. W. Munsell, 1887.

Bagg, Lyman, *Four Years At Yale,* New Haven, Charles C. Chatfield & Co., 1871.

Dahl, Robert A., *Who Governs? Democracy and Power in an American City,* New Haven, Yale University Press, 1961.

Dana, Arnold G., *New Haven's Problems: Whither the City? All Cities?* New Haven, Tuttle, Morehouse and Taylor, 1937.

De Forest, John William, *History of the Indians of Connecticut from the Earliest Known Period to 1850.* Published with the sanction of the Connecticut Historical Society, Hartford, W. J. Hamersley, 1851.

Goals for New Haven, Inc., Committee Reports, New Haven, 1979.

Hill, Everett G., *A Modern History of New Haven and Eastern New Haven County,* New York, S. J. Clark Publishing Co., 1918.

Hornstein, Harold, ed., *New Haven Celebrates the Bicentennial,* New Haven, The New Haven Bicentennial Commission, 1976.

Johnston, William Michael, "On the Outside Looking In: Irish, Italian and Black Ethnic Politics in an American City," Yale Ph.D. Dissertation, 1977.

Knight, Sarah Kemble, *The Journals of Madam Knight, and Rev. Mr. Buckingham, From the Original Manuscript, Written in 1704 & 1710,* New York, Wilder & Campbell, 1825.

Levermore, Charles H., *The Republic of New Haven: A History of Municipal Evolution,* Baltimore, Johns Hopkins University Press, 1886.

Lewis, Sinclair, "Young Man Axelbrod," in *Selected Short Stories of Sinclair Lewis,* Garden City, New York, Doubleday, Doran & Co., 1935. See also: Arthur A. Chiel, "Sinclair Lewis at Yale," *Yale Alumni Magazine,* vol. 40, Dec. 1976, pp. 38, 39.

Osterweis, Rollin G., *Three Centuries of New Haven, 1638–1938,* New Haven, Yale University Press, 1953.

Schiff, Judith A., "Colonel Isaac Ullman: Philanthropist, Politician, and Patriot," *Jews in New Haven* II: 32–40, New Haven, The Jewish Historical Society of New Haven, 1979.

Seymour, George Dudley, *New Haven,* New Haven, privately printed, 1942.

Silliman, Benjamin, "Reminiscences," Silliman Family Papers, Yale University Library. Quoted in Judith A. Schiff, "Benjamin Silliman (1779–1864): A 200th Birthday Celebration Honoring the Father of American Scientific Education," *Yale University Library Gazette,* vol. 54, pp. 149–162, April 1980.

Terry, Harriett Wadsworth. Letter to her sisters, 1887, June 18, Terry Family Papers, Yale University Library.

Warner, Robert Austin, *New Haven Negroes: A Social History,* New Haven, Yale University Press, 1940.

Yale University. *Yale and New Haven: A Study of the Benefits Derived Locally from an Endowed University,* New Haven, Yale University, 1937.

Yale University, Class of 1874, *Histories,* New Haven, Tuttle, Morehouse & Taylor, 1877–1919. Biographical material relating to Edward Bouchet.

Chapter VI Notes

[1] Knight, *The Journals of Madam Knight,* p. 36.

[2] *Ibid.,* p. 40.

[3] *Ibid.*

[4] *Ibid.*

[5] De Forest, *History of the Indians of Connecticut,* pp. 162, 163.

Chapter VIII References

Atwater, Edward Elias, and others, *History of the City of New Haven to the Present Time,* New York, W. W. Munsell & Co., 1887.

Bartlett, Ellen Strong, *Historic Sketches of New Haven,* New Haven, privately published, 1897.

Brown, Elizabeth Mills, *New Haven: A Guide to Architecture and Urban Design,* New Haven, Yale University Press, 1976. This invaluable guidebook with its thoughtful foreword is the definitive treatise on the history of New Haven architecture. The author of this chapter appreciates Mrs. Brown's permission to draw from her book and much of the material in this chapter has been derived from it.

Brown, Elizabeth Mills, with Townsend, Doris B., *Wooster Square and Its Historic Architecture, 1825–1880,* with accompanying portfolio *Historic Houses of Wooster Square,* New Haven, New Haven Preservation Trust, 1969.

Carroll, Richard C., *Buildings and Grounds of Yale University,* New Haven, Yale University Printing Service, 1979.

Dana, Arnold Guyot, *New Haven Old and New,* New Haven, New Haven Colony Historical Society, Mss. No. 1, undated.

Getlein, Edward J., *Here Will I Dwell,*

A history of Trinity Church-on-the-Green, New Haven, Trinity Church, 1976.

Kelly, J. Frederick, *Early Connecticut Meeting Houses*, New York, Columbia University Press, 1948. Volume II.

Osterweis, Rollin, *Three Centuries of New Haven, 1638–1938*, New Haven, Yale University Press, 1953.

Peck, Henry H., *The New Haven State House*, New Haven, Peck and G. H. Coe, 1889.

Seymour, George Dudley, *New Haven*, New Haven, privately printed, 1942.

Exhibition catalog, *A Graphic View of New Haven*, New Haven, New Haven Colony Historical Society, 1976.

Selections from the Historic American Buildings Survey, National Park Service, Division of Historic Architecture, *New Haven Architecture*, Washington, D.C., U.S. Government Printing Office, 1970.

Original Sources

Austin, Henry. Architectural drawings and renderings, New Haven, Manuscripts and Archives, Sterling Memorial Library, Yale University.

Austin, Henry; Brown, David R.; Mitchell, Donald Grant; Russell, Rufus; Town, Ithiel; and others. Architectural drawings and renderings, New Haven, New Haven Colony Historical Society.

Banner, Peter. Certain cost estimates and drawings, New Haven, Manuscripts and Archives, Sterling Memorial Library, Yale University.

Davis, Alexander Jackson. Plans, exterior elevations and renderings of interiors of "Sachem's Wood," New Haven, Manuscripts and Archives, Sterling Memorial Library, Yale University.

Orr, Douglas W. Job files 1926-1966, New Haven, Douglas Orr, Winder and Associates.

Tiffany, Louis Comfort and LaFarge, John. Art glass windows in Center Church, New Haven, Center Church records.

INDEX

THIS BOOK WAS TYPESET IN
PALATINO
PRINTED ON 80LB.
ENAMEL
AND BOUND BY
WALSWORTH PUBLISHING
COMPANY.
COVER AND TEXT DESIGNED
BY
ALEXANDER D'ANCA
LAYOUT BY
JAMES METROPOLE AND
DON GOULD